How to live like a Chipmunk
and other tips on

Living an Awesome Sauce Life

PATTY LOWRY

BALBOA
PRESS
A DIVISION OF HAY HOUSE

Copyright © 2016 Patty Lowry.
Cover Design/ Interior Graphics/Art Credit: Chris Abbott

All rights reserved. No part of this book may be used or reproduced by any means, graphic, electronic, or mechanical, including photocopying, recording, taping or by any information storage retrieval system without the written permission of the author except in the case of brief quotations embodied in critical articles and reviews.

Balboa Press books may be ordered through booksellers or by contacting:

Balboa Press
A Division of Hay House
1663 Liberty Drive
Bloomington, IN 47403
www.balboapress.com
1 (877) 407-4847

Because of the dynamic nature of the Internet, any web addresses or links contained in this book may have changed since publication and may no longer be valid. The views expressed in this work are solely those of the author and do not necessarily reflect the views of the publisher, and the publisher hereby disclaims any responsibility for them.

The author of this book does not dispense medical advice or prescribe the use of any technique as a form of treatment for physical, emotional, or medical problems without the advice of a physician, either directly or indirectly. The intent of the author is only to offer information of a general nature to help you in your quest for emotional and spiritual well-being. In the event you use any of the information in this book for yourself, which is your constitutional right, the author and the publisher assume no responsibility for your actions.

Any people depicted in stock imagery provided by Thinkstock are models, and such images are being used for illustrative purposes only.
Certain stock imagery © Thinkstock.

Print information available on the last page.

ISBN: 978-1-5043-5367-0 (sc)
ISBN: 978-1-5043-5368-7 (hc)
ISBN: 978-1-5043-5369-4 (e)

Library of Congress Control Number: 2016904308

Balboa Press rev. date: 4/28/2016

About the Author

Patty Lowry is part pixie, part philosopher and part warrior princess! Imagine if Nancy Drew and Mary Richards had a ménage à trois with Agent Scully, while Peggy Olson took notes. Ahem.

Award-winning copywriter at a super cool advertising agency (by day) and joyful, magical and adventurous moxie-maker (by night), Patty's claim to fame is Brownie of the Year, 1969. She is a self-described forest-frolicking hippie who loves nature above all else.

> "The elements are my messengers. My imagination is my compass and wanderlust is my path." - Patty

Contents

Dedication xi
Preface xiii
High Fives xv
Introduction xvii
How to live like a chipmunk. xix

HAPPY STUFF 1

JOY 3
    How to be happy 4
    How to choose happiness 5
    How to make someone feel good 6
    How to be wonder full★ 7
    How to engage your inner child 8
    How to be positive 9
    How to have fun 10
    How to manifest your dreams 11

WHOLENESS 13
    How to be yourself 14
    How to be confident 15
    How to be grateful 16
    How to be spirit full★ 17
    How to be vulnerable 18
    How to be empathetic 19
    How to be a better person 20
    How to be sickeningly nice 21
    How to discover your purpose 22
    How to get your magic moxie★ back 23

SUPER SKILLS 25
How to be uber cool 26
How to be OMFG creative 27
How to surprise people 28
How to be adventurous 29
How to be organized 30
How to slow down 31
How to relax 32
How to meditate 33

GOOD TO KNOW 35
How to buy a home and be a homeowner 36
How to be crafty (in a good way) 38
How to throw an awesome party 39
How to be a pet owner 40
How to be eco-friendly 42

LOVE 45
How to love yourself 46
How to fall in love 47
How to find true love 48
How to flirt 49
How to feel sexy 50

NATURE 53
How to be one with nature 54
How to communicate with animals, bugs and birds 55
How to travel off the beaten path 56

STRESSY STUFF 59

FEAR 61
How to break through insurmountable fear 62
How to manage unreasonable stress 63
How to cope with anxiety 64
How to have faith in the unknown 65
How to manage a bad case of the nerves 66
How to let go of worry 67

INNER STRENGTH ... 69
- How to cope with being broken ... 70
- How to cope when you're not ... 71
- How to keep yourself motivated ... 72
- How to trust and be trusted ... 73
- How to forgive ... 74
- How to let go ... 75
- How to stand up for yourself ... 76
- How to disarm insecurity ... 77
- How to be honest with yourself ... 78

SADNESS ... 81
- How to cope with regret ... 82
- How to not feel lonely ... 83
- How to get over disappointment ... 84
- How to cheer yourself up ... 85

ANGER ... 87
- How to handle anger, fury and wrath ... 88
- How to find patience when there isn't a drop left ... 89

SUPER SKILLS ... 91
- How to process the loss of your parents ... 92
- How to deal with family ... 94
- How to love the meanie ... 95
- How to do something that you really don't want to do ... 96
- How to age gracefully and never grow old ... 97
- How to be a grown-up (aka do the right thing.) ... 98

GOOD TO KNOW 101
    How to get some perspective 102
    How to create calm 104
    How to deal with boredom 105
    How to stop being a control freak 106
    How to not cheat when dieting 107
    How to cope with a being in a drunken stupor 108
    How to cope with a juicy cold 109
    How to embrace exercise 110
    How to save money when you are broke 111
    How to rock a resumé, ace an interview
    and be employee of the month 112
    How to ask your boss for a raise 113

LOVE 115
    How to heal a broken heart 116
    How to break up with someone 117
    How to survive/succeed at online dating 118
    How to go on a date after not being on a date in ages 120
    How to love yourself when you are having an
    "I'm fat, ugly, stupid AND a bad hair day" day 121

LAST BUT NOT LEAST 123
    How to make Awesome Sauce 124

PATTY-ISMS 127

PATTY-ISMS ★: Made up words and phrases with real meanings
that are way more fun than the real words that inspired them 128

YOU'RE A WINNER! 131
    A BONUS peek into Patty's nature and lessons learned 132

Dedication

To the one and only magical Kate Sharpe: thanks for teaching me that "Julie isn't real" and to believe that if I unlock the vault, anything is possible.

Preface

OK, take a seat; I'm going to share a super big secret. A secret that I've hidden with shame for most of my life. I've pretended, camouflaged, covered up, overcompensated and fooled the masses for decades…but of late, I've decided to come clean, embrace it, own it, love it, pet it, hug it and squeeze it. Are you ready?

I struggle with words: I'm dyslexic. I suck at spelling, I'm lousy at grammar and, frankly, I have no real affection for punctuation, periods or proper prose for that matter.

When I was little the teacher called me stupid. I had to go to the "special" class. Little did they know that being "special" would reveal some pretty awesome sauce perks. Perks that included having my parents tell me that I was born on a star and that I had secret super powers. Perks that trained me to infuse my imagination with uber effervescent sparkle. Perks that led me to hone in on and celebrate my own unique way of expressing my observations, ideas and feelings. Perks that made me wonderfully peculiar…and ironically helped me to become a very clever and creative writer. Still, I held onto the identity of "being stupid," not good enough and not smart enough to write a book.

Then one day, not too long ago and not without a heap of heavy lifting of massive boulders, I decided to leave that cave. I am smart. Not because I have a degree or an exceptionally high IQ. Not because I comprehend algebra or know how to program my thermostat or spell tchotchke (seriously…as if).

I am smart because I am resourceful (Brownie of the Year, 1969). I am smart because I have an open heart and an imagination that is full of possibilities. And I am smart because I'm curious and covet as many experiences and emotions as I can so that I can learn from them and say that I have lived life to the fullest.

So I wrote this book. I dared myself to do it and, more importantly, to do it my way. Now I am going to share it. For two reasons – one, if it can make even the most molecular difference in someone's day – make them smile, think, have hope or find joy – then I will be happy. And two – to give a shout out to anyone who has been told that they aren't smart enough. I want to let you know that you are smart enough. Own your own light.

xx Patty

High Fives

I have always fantasized about winning an Oscar. Not because I'm an actor (although I do dream about starring in a film alongside Robert Downey Jr. an awful lot), but more so because it's an incredible opportunity to express thanks… and to wear a sparkly dress.

So, in dramatic Oscar-like fashion, with delicate tears trickling down my amazed face, holding on tightly to my little golden man, I'd like to thank a few peeps, whom without their brilliance, supportiveness and inspiration I wouldn't be celebrating this big girl accomplishment.

Mom & Dad: man oh man do I ever love you and miss you. Thanks for making me feel like I could do anything – from trying out for cheerleading and leads in school musicals to travelling the world and earning my wings. Most of all, thanks for not listening to that teacher who said I was stupid. Thanks for only seeing my unique abilities and for encouraging me to think differently, experience the world differently and to use my imagination as my super power.

To my tribe of fellow friends and freaks…shanks sistahs and brothers: thanks for playing with me, putting up with me, inspiring me and loving me – I loviate yous to the moon and beyond.

To the teacher who called me stupid, the mean girls, bad bosses and people who broke my heart: thank you so much for challenging me and helping me to learn some really big lessons. I'm a much wiser person for knowing you.

To the brilliantly talented Chris Abbott: thank you so much for your friendship and awesome sauce magical work on my cover and inside pages.

To my darling friend Mike Dineen: you truly have the most beautiful mind and spirit. I marvel at your smarty pants molecules and so appreciate all your wordy wisdom and wordsmithing.

Ask and the universe will deliver. My proof is Eleanor Healy. A "chance" meeting which has led to a new friendship and incredible support to help me "love, pet, hug and squeeze" (aka edit) my baby.

And last but not least, to all the faeries living in the chandelier: thank you guys for never leaving me, even when I felt like the magic did…I will always believe!

Introduction

How to Live Like a Chipmunk and Other Tips on Living an Awesome Sauce Life.

> *"Life can be wonderful, amazing and funny and it can also be hard, scary and full of surprises…if only there was a manual! Just a simple guide to show me how to get from point A to point B (in the quickest and least painful way)." - Patty*

If you've ever uttered those words, then this book is for you! Perfect for time-challenged peeps who want to make their life better NOW instead of later!

A handy-dandy, cut to the chase, tell it to me simple, real life "how-to" guide for all the different situations that life throws at you. You'll find over eighty instructional lists for both celebratory and challenging life scenarios; including everything from how to handle a bad hair day and broken heart to how to be the best you.

This love-your-life guide is jam-packed with smart, sincere, sarcastic and saucy – awesome saucy, that is – sensibilities that are true to the core and straight to the point. Eleven points to be exact. Eleven because 10 steps are doable and one more for good luck.

So what's my point and what's up with the chipmunk?

My adventure started with a quest for answers. A key to unlock my emotional vault. Sure, there are volumes of books out there, really long books…they made nice doorstops.

You see I have the patience of a flea; I want the answers now. I also share the high-spirited, hyper multi-tasking, practical productiveness of a chipmunk. We are inquisitive and intuitive, resourceful and relentless and we are both driven by the desire to find the quickest path to the peanut.

In an effort to simplify, shorten and sweeten my path to emotional freedom, I gathered and collected all my nutty nuggets of wisdom, wit, woes and whimsical worldliness at a chipmunk's pace, added to the mix my lust for lists and – in a nutshell – I present you with the quickest path to the peanut.

There are many ways to search for nuts and many paths to wander in the forest of life. This is the path that I took. I am not a guru; I am simply a girl, a warrior and a winner. I drank the Kool-Aid, read all the garrulous self-help books, did the damned exercises, dug the dirt, laid in the grave, sweated the details, swung the sword, climbed the fricking mountain, fell off it, broke into a million pieces, and eventually I found my way back again. I've earned my badges, my authenticity and my truth.

These are my how-tos. They are derived from personal experience, motivated by an oath to be real and intended to spark a smile. My hope is that they will provide you with a plethora of new possibilities, debunk the ordinary, amp up the extraordinary and offer up options for you to live your most awesome sauce life.

Curious? Good clever monkey! Scared? Don't worry…there's a chapter on that! Choose to cartwheel into the colourful corridors of a warrior princess's mindscapes and discover pearls of wisdom and petals of magic. Explore this guide with abandon: play, ponder and choose your own path.

P.S. Seeing stars ★ ? Don't worry…it's just a Patty-ism! Throughout my book you will encounter words that I made up. Dad always said if you say them enough, people would start to use them. There is a glossary at the back of the book to help you unveil their meanings.

How to live like a chipmunk.

1. Live small and simply.
2. Gather resources for a rainy day, a wintry day…or a Tuesday.
3. Always stop and smell the acorns.
4. Choose cute and cuddly over nasty and gnarly.
5. Make nice with your furry and feathered friends.
6. Be grateful for small things…like peanuts.
7. Learn to trust humans…and squirrels.
8. Be one with nature.
9. Don't let anyone call you a rodent.
10. Always keep a tidy home.
11. Let your adorable, lively, brave and quirky personality shine through.

How to be happy.

1. Be you. You're already the most awesome sauce YOU in the entire universe galaxy! Shake your pom-poms baby!
2. NEVER listen to naysayers, bosses who are drunk by lunch, teachers who call you dumb, parents who worry that you're destined to be a secretary or scaredy-cat wannabees with inflated egos of their dullard reality. ALWAYS listen to strangers on the bus who talk to you or themselves, children, animals and the voices (I know you hear them too).
3. Trust your gut instinct. It tells you the truth 99% of the time. Your gut instinct creates a wonderful and peaceful feeling as opposed to the nauseous ache of the horror-filled ego – which feels like the time you ate an entire family-sized bag of ripple chips with onion dip, washed down with a bottle of red wine.
4. Make stuff up to validate your beliefs. Name your pet unicorn!
5. Be fearless. Feel Everything And Rejoice! Shake hands with your horror stories, give them a hug, have a drink with them – then make a monster face and tell them to get out (Amityville Horror style).
6. Don't play it safe. Crazy spontaneity and imaginative combustion is way more fun and it's also contagious!
7. Replace the word need with desire.
8. Embrace mayhem, madness and chaos – it is a prerequisite in the process of evolution.
9. Believe in something unbelievable, invisible and intangible.
10. Embrace your inner psychopath. Don't act on it – just tend to it.
11. Lose the attitude. Develop a lovitude ★.

How to choose happiness.

1. Start with smiling. It's easy and only takes 17 muscles as opposed to the 43 that it takes to frown.
2. Count your blessings: be grateful for what is yours.
3. Don't compare yourself to others. Life isn't always what it seems to be on the outside and studies show that if you put all your friends' problems in a pot, you'd pick your own.
4. Always believe that something wonderful is about to happen. Optimism is a natural breeding ground for joy.
5. Choose it! Happiness is a choice. It's an option. Happiness can be your outlook, perspective, attitude and altitude.
6. Happiness isn't a constant state of being. There has to be both rainy and sunny days. Just try not to let the bumpy days linger. Feel. Deal. Heal. Work through your worry, anger, disappointment, sadness and hurt. Forgive, let go and make peace.
7. Think happy to create happy. Plant giggles, memories, dreams, wishes and joyful jellybeans of glee in your mind. Paint your walls orange, wear yellow and surround yourself with molecules of magic, beauty and joy.
8. Do what makes you happy. Dance, sing, make art, crank the tunes, cook, laugh, play and always be true to yourself.
9. Money doesn't buy you happiness but being comfortable with your bills and lifestyle contributes to a happier you. Budget your coin responsibly so you have some leftover to play with.
10. Invest in friendships. Get a pet. Share. Do something nice for yourself and for someone else.
11. Do the hokey-pokey, hum, toss lucky pennies into the street and for goodness' sake – wear your rainbow wings.

How to make someone feel good.

1. Make an effort to know what their favourite things are.
2. Surprise them with a coffee, donut or unicorn sticker.
3. Acknowledge their birthday, good hair day, cool outfit or smarty-pants effort.
4. Pay attention to them. Listen to them. Be interested. Remember stuff they say. Ask questions. Give a shit.
5. Let them into your world. Rant, rave, smile and share.
6. Be the first to say "good morning", "hi", "how ya doing?" or "I'm sorry".
7. Send an email, make a phone call, leave a smiley post-it note.
8. Do random gestures of kindness…just because.
9. Put their needs first. Have their back. Be their cheerleader.
10. Smile, hug them, make them laugh or do an interpretive dance to express your feelings for them (aka make them laugh).
11. Make them feel like they matter. BTW – everyone matters.

How to be wonder full★.

1. Be insatiably curious. Find out what's in that secret locked closet. Dip pickles in butterscotch and discover what makes an elephant giggle.
2. Dare yourself on a daily basis.
3. Imagine the unimaginable.
4. Covet brand-spanking new experiences, strange strangers, awkward situations and out-of-the-box, out-of-your-mind adventures.
5. Choose the path less travelled and get lost.
6. Expect the unexpected.
7. Amp up your molecular adrenaline. Surprise, shock and mildly scardiate★ people. Keep them guessing.
8. Be remarkable. Save worms on the pavement.
9. Admire someone and live up to their super star status.
10. Experience life to the fullest. Suck a jellybean until each grain of ambrosial-infused sugar dissolves, sending your senses into a candy euphoria!
11. Hunt for the pot of gold at the rainbow's end. Reach for the stars on your tippy-toes, oh so high. Trust that when you least expect to find it…you will.

How to engage your inner child.

1. Wrap a towel around your head and pretend that it's your hair.
2. Throw a temper tantrum. Even better – do it in public.
3. For starters – rock your pigtails, jump in puddles, walk like a penguin, eat peanut butter, grapes & hotdog sandwiches and always colour outside the lines.
4. Reunite with your invisible best friend. I love you, Bobo!
5. Wear polka dots and stripes at the same time and add bunny ears for a little extra flair.
6. Embrace everything like it's your first time.
7. Believe in the unbelievable: Santa, The Easter Bunny, Unicorns and The Tooth Faerie.
8. Play more. Visit a farm. Go to the zoo. Talk to a squirrel. Write a story. Draw a picture. Make macaroni art.
9. Let your silly out. Spontaneously dance, sing, do a cartwheel or stuff marshmallows in your mouth.
10. Let your imagination run wild. Go on a safari with your pet flying monkey. Visit Mars in your spaceship. Swim in a sky of stars as a mermaid. Talk to the faeries in the chandelier.
11. Embrace wonder, joy, innocence and the monsters under the bed.

How to be positive.

1. Choose between being a collection of happy, shiny, rainbow-magic jellybean molecules of effervescent-infused joy or mud girl★.
2. See beauty, fortune, wonder and magic everywhere. Look for it in nature's colours, scents and sounds, fluffy clouds, resilient trees, singing birds, random squirrels, quirky architecture, tossed-out treasures, people's faces, funky outfits, and anything else that strikes your fancy. Just take notice!
3. Count what you have, not what you don't have.
4. See the field, not the fence.
5. Life's a mystery, so assume that it's a box of kittens and not a box of scorpions.
6. Make it your regular practice. Aim to be friendly, nice, complimentary and joyful towards yourself, the snarky bus driver, the adorable, but stinky screaming baby on the bus, the oblivious too-cool-for-school backpack boy, the stream of slow walkers on the stairs, seat-hoggers on the subway, the 99 year old lady in line ordering coffee and trying to decide what donut she wants, your coworkers (especially the yucky ones), your boss, any irritating family members, friends and unfriendly random squirrels. Do it all day and see what happens. Betcha get it back!
7. Embrace the magic notion that what you think and do will result in how you will feel and what you will receive.
8. Don't compare yourself to anything or anyone. Your life is yours and it's what you make of it. If you want a better job, a bigger bank account or to be a supermodel or astronaut – then do it.
9. Nothing is perfect. Life is bumpy. Sometimes we don't win. Redefine the "ouchies" as life lessons. Look for the good in every situation and in every person – even if the only good that you can find is the lesson of patience.
10. Fake it until you make it. Act as if you already are Pollyanna on Prozac... it's a habit in the making and it's very contagious.
11. Helpful quotes, affirmations, mottos and post-it notes: "Beauty is as beauty does." "Blessed are the cracked for they let in the most light." "Feck Perfuction." "This too shall pass." "Take things one day at a time." "You are more than enough."

How to have fun.

1. Let go of control, the shouldn'ts, the don'ts and the pressure of being a grown-up. Be sure to break the rules!
2. Be spontaneous! Jump in the sprinkler, make a snow angel or start a dance party on the street. Own your Silly Billy!
3. Dress the part! Pull out your tutu, faerie wings and sparkly sneakers.
4. Dare to do something different. Go to a rodeo, learn pole dancing, swim with the sharks or take up axe throwing.
5. Laugh – at comedians, movies, each other and especially yourself.
6. Throw a come-as-you-are potluck pyjama party.
7. Be the first to sing, dance and dress like a full on freak, because everyone is waiting for permission to do the same.
8. Explore nature. Watch bugs, climb a tree, go on a picnic, splash in the water, dig in the dirt, roll in the leaves and howl at the moon.
9. Play Bingo, Charades or Truth, Dare or Double Dare! Swing a bat, kick a ball and bluff your way through a hand of poker! Pull out Twister, your Hot Wheels set or play hide and go seek. Be a child again.
10. Do something that you love to do. Cook, garden, make music, art – even better, do it with fun people.
11. Play make believe and choose to see everything as an adventure.

How to manifest your dreams.

1. Believe beyond a shadow of a doubt that you can do it. You can!
2. Create a mantra and say it 100 times a day. For example, "I own a petting zoo." "I own a petting zoo." "I own a petting zoo."
3. Plant seeds the size of coconuts. Everywhere. Tend to them daily.
4. Reframe everything that you think and say as though it is happening in this moment. "I love playing with my pet monkey Mervin." "I love the rainbow monkey barn."
5. Commit to your dreams. Come up with a theme song, a daily ritual, post-it notes of affirmations and a treasure box to store all of your super cool ideas and clippings. Practice doing things you thought were impossible every day.
6. Have real conversations with your imaginary dream team (and animals).
7. Star in the block buster movie version of your life.
8. Tell everyone what you are going to do. Backer-outers suck.
9. When it feels really far away – look over the fence and into the field of daisies. See, it's not that far after all.
10. Draw a map. Establish signposts. Set milestones. Treat yourself to good hiking boots because you're going to go far!
11. Recruit believers.

How to be yourself.

1. Start with loving yourself from head-to-toe, inside out and upside down.
2. Don't second-guess it. Just be you.
3. Own your unique pizzazz. From freckles and Bozo the clown curls to wonky winks, wiggles and giggles – it's all YOU!
4. Love the skin that you're in. Love every inch, jiggle, wrinkle and curve.
5. Do what makes you happy. Talk to squirrels, wear your mermaid tail and love Taylor Swift!
6. Claim your fashion fame. Rock the fun-fur jumpsuit, sparkly cape and pink cowgirl go-go boots. Define your personal style!
7. Celebrate your own identity and celebrity status. There's no need to mimic, impersonate or copy anyone else. You rock.
8. Master your multiple personalities! Contemplate the notion that "the self" can evolve and change. Think about who you want to be.
9. Always choose quirky over perfection.
10. Don't give a poop about what other people think. You want to be liked for being the real you, not the people-pleasing pretend you.
11. Shine your light from the inside out.

How to be confident.

1. Fake it until you make it. Start small and reward yourself with gold stars.
2. How you think affects how you feel and in turn, will affect how you act.
3. Learn to rely on yourself. Remember when you fell down – you got up!
4. Affirmations and declarations equal liberation!
5. Accept that nothing is certain (except how you choose to handle a situation). Choose strength.
6. Practice and prepare. From body language to verbal language. Write conversations, speeches and soliloquies. Grab your hairbrush and stand in front of the mirror. Get friendly with your fear then stand up straight and make eye contact!
7. Who is the best you? You are. Know your strengths and weaknesses.
8. Claim your own style with confidence. Not everyone is a Johnny Depp or a Martha Stewart. Wear your super cape with pride.
9. Foster trademarks of confidence like spunk, pluck, moxie, humour, sarcasm, wit, stillness, silence, poise, boldness, backbone and grit.
10. Accept compliments. Stockpile praise. Expect success.
11. Never forget that you matter. A lot.

How to be grateful.

1. Count your blessings. It can always be worse.
2. Compare your first world problem to third world problems.
3. Do you have a roof over your head? Food in your fridge? Clothes on your back? Enough said.
4. So what if your job is stressful? It's not called work for nothing.
5. Embrace the habit of acknowledging your gratitude. Start a gratitude diary. List five things every day that you are grateful for. For example, my freckles, my pets, the sunshine, the delicious banana I had for breakfast and a blue sky.
6. Do good deeds and random acts of kindness. It's contagious and Karma will love you for it.
7. Be grateful out loud. Tell your friends and family how much they mean to you. Express gratitude to the stranger who gives you a seat on the bus. Say thank you and mean it.
8. Get with the grateful mindset. Acknowledge and accept. See the silver lining – even challenges can be awesome life lessons.
9. Avoid negativity, giving in to jealousy and complaining. Choose positivity, contentment and grace.
10. Appreciate the moment. Life can change on a dime.
11. Savour the sweet spots. Share when your cup runneth over. Always give thanks.

How to be spirit full★.

1. Be aware and thankful for the abundance in your life.
2. Your spirit is your natural essence – a combination of your emotions, character and soul. Your true self. Your most magical being. Be your best being.
3. Gawd★ Gawddess, Buddha, Allah, Ganesh; Judaism, Hinduism, Christianity, Taoism, Islam, Paganism; angels, faeries, bunny heaven, mermaids and unicorns. Call it what you will. If you believe, it's real.
4. You can call it religion, a higher power, spirituality, philosophy, agnosticism, pragmatism, universal love, magic or being a believer – if it works for you keep doing it.
5. Faith is personal. Believe in and trust what resonates with you and gives meaning to your life. It's all good.
6. Express your spirit with praise, thanks, good words, good wishes and good deeds.
7. Foster your spirit. Fill up on it. Let it light your heart and mind, then let it loose! Dance, sing, share and rejoice in whatever way works for you!
8. Celebrate your spirit! Go to festivals, feasts and bon fires. And definitely wear costumes!
9. Get naked! It's your best "super natural" being.
10. G.O.D. – Great. Out. Doors.
11. Breathe it. Believe it. Be it.

How to be vulnerable.

1. Being open to censure, criticism, hurt, harm and temptation also prepares you to be open to approval, applause, freedom, joy, adventure and love.
2. Accept that no one, including and especially you, is unbreakable and I don't recommend falling down the stairs to prove it.
3. Put aside your moxie-assed mule, super control freak, self-governing, independent attitude and admit that you could use a little itty bit of help…just maybe.
4. Crack open the vault and reach down into the subterranean caverns of your defensive soul to pull out your bare naked, un-armoured, shelter less self. Easy peasy right?
5. Relinquish being Super Woman, Helen Keller, Joan of Arc or Maria from the Sound of Music.
6. Learn to ask for help. "You know that 100 lb pile of logs? Oh, did I mention that I'm baking brownies on Saturday?"
7. Shift your paradigm. Asking for help doesn't mean that you're helpless – it means you're human. In fact, if you ask that cute strong lumberjack to help you move the logs you might possibly kill two birds with one stone.
8. When you feel stupid, needy, weak or less awesome than usual, remember that these feelings are normal – everyone experiences those feelings at some point. Join the club!
9. When people ask how you're feeling try answering with something other than the word "fine". For example, you can reply, "I feel like the weight of 10,000 pregnant rhinos are stomping on my bleeding shattered heart."
10. Showing your vulnerability takes trust and practice. Give it a try around those you trust, like your cat. "Angus I want to share how I feel about you barfing on my pillow."
11. Being vulnerable means that you have to be cool with all the parts of you…both the shiny and the dark bits. When you're being authentic you can accept yourself for who you really are. And that's a beautiful thing.

How to be empathetic.

1. Try on other people's shoes, jackets and hats. Swap life stories for a day.
2. Count your blessings and share them, especially if they're buttertarts.
3. Grasp the notion of reciprocity: "you must give love to receive love".
4. Ask yourself what Gandhi, Buddha or Winnie-the-Pooh would do?
5. Hello, Karma! What goes around comes around. Ask yourself how you would like to be treated, cared for, listened to?
6. Understand the difference between listening to someone and trying to fix their problems and offering someone compassion versus pity.
7. Bite your lip or put tape over your mouth when a friend bares their soul. It's not about sharing advice, it's about sharing silent space.
8. Listen with your ears, eyes and heart. Try not to fidget, roll your eyes or emit frustrated noises. Come on, you can do it. I know it's really hard sometimes.
9. Sometimes gestures speak louder than words. Did someone say buttertarts?!
10. If you've been there then be there. From broken hearts and bad hair days to feeling stupid, fat, afraid and alone. If you've felt the pain then share the love.
11. Brownie Badge #23: this is what we do as elves, think of others, not just ourselves." Empathizing expands your capacity for love.

How to be a better person.

1. Find a role model like Mother Teresa, Gandhi, Nancy Drew or Scooby Doo. Then you can aspire to their awesome sauciness★.
2. Give back and forth and upside down. Volunteer. Do charity work. Donate time, money and hugs.
3. Suck it up, Buttercup. Say sorry first. Forgive yourself and others.
4. Give up your seat. Hold open a door. Say please & thank you. Manners do matter.
5. Do random acts of spontaneous kindness all over the place. Put on a happy face every day, everywhere and in every moment.
6. Share your candy.
7. Pick up the tab.
8. Empathize with others. Treat people how you would like to be treated.
9. Be humble. You don't always have to be right; tuck away that ego.
10. Stop making excuses. Just fricking do it. It will feel wonderful.
11. Your beliefs don't make you a better person – your behaviour does.

How to be sickeningly nice.

1. Suck up to the meanie.
2. Embrace your inner Pollyanna.
3. Love your enemies (it drives them crazy).
4. Two wrongs don't make a right. Two rights make a friend.
5. Be the better person. Extend the olive branch. If you can't say anything nice – don't say anything. Don't give them a reason to retaliate.
6. Remember that KARMA gets you every time.
7. Be polite, say thank you and please, smile at noisy children, help old people (you'll be old one day), talk to animals, hold doors open, give up your seat, don't push and always say "have a nice day".
8. If you want more love you have to give more love. Everyone wants to feel as though they matter.
9. Aim to do five good deeds per day. Get them done by noon, so that you're free to be naughty for the rest of the day!
10. Give compliments. Nice neon eye shadow you're wearing! Love what you did with your bald spot! Bumblebee stripes are so slimming on you! Man! You're rocking that forehead tattoo! Who would have thought a forehead tattoo rocks!
11. Treat people how you want to be treated.

How to discover your purpose.

1. Lift the veil of illusion to reveal the possibilities. Ask yourself what you would do if you could do anything. Would you be a petting zoo owner, movie star or Unicorns Unlimited shop owner?
2. Make a list of what makes you feel the happiest. What tickles your brain and your heart? Identify your talents, skills, passions and gifts.
3. Read "Oh, the places you'll go" by Dr. Seuss.
4. Think about what you wanted to be when you were a child.
5. Think about the reasons why you do what you do - in life and in work. How does it make you feel? Does it feel natural? Happy? Contrived? Fake?
6. What's the first thing you think of when you wake up in the morning? Are you excited about your day? You should be. You can be.
7. Make a list of the people you admire and why.
8. Interview yourself or pretend you are on a talk show. What inspires you? Moves you? Comforts you? Makes you go hmmm?
9. Write your personal mantra, motto or mission. JOY! MAGIC! ADVENTURE!
10. What do you give a damn about? What matters so much to you that you'd stand on a pedestal and yell it out to the world? I dare you to do it!
11. Start with baby steps. It's all about momentum. Imagine one domino that wants desperately to move forward. Then visualize a whole congregation of dominoes that only need a tiny nudge to get the ball rolling. Nothing can stop you now!

How to get your magic moxie★ back.

1. You must want it. Really, really, REALLY badly.
2. Foster it. Set a place for it. Invite it to hang out. Love it and pet it and hug it and squeeze it.
3. Be brave. It can be a battle to bring it out again, but it's a fight worth winning.
4. Make up a magic moxie mantra: I AM A MAGICAL RAINBOW CHILD OF LOVE. THIS IS MY TIME. I LOVE THE SHIT OUTTA EVERYTHING.
5. Put on your super cape, sparkly cowgirl boots and tiara and hop onto your rainbow unicorn! Let the journey begin! If you fall off the unicorn, get back on it.
6. See the field of daisies. I mean really see it. It may be in the distance but you can still head in that direction. Stop at nothing to get to the field. Hop fences, dig tunnels, go through the mud, get dirty, get clean; keep your eye on the prize. Soon you'll be rolling in the daisies.
7. Focus on yourself. What are your wants, needs, desires, wishes, cravings and absolutely must-haves?
8. Fill up your magic cups: your body, heart, mind, spirit, creativity, curiosity, sociability, emotional and inspirational mugs of love.
9. Let it happen. Lower the drawbridge, lift the veil and open the windows and doors of your soul. Say yes, please and thank you to your magic moxie.
10. Call upon your magic charms.
11. Abracadabra. Hocus-pocus. Alakazam. BELIEVE in yourself.

Super Skills

How to be uber cool.

1. Old school is always cool. Duh.
2. What goes around comes around, except for the unitard.
3. Know that a pretentiously named colour that is a shade of black is NOT the new black.
4. Don't follow the pack – lead your own gaggle.
5. Be full of surprises. Throw curveballs.
6. Be a cherub on the outside and a mad trickster on the inside.
7. Be really awesome at something like hopscotch, hula-hooping or pogo-sticking.
8. Create a signature expression…loviation★.
9. Perfect your cartwheel.
10. Collect things such as bug wings, eggcups, wind-up toys, belt buckles, berets or all of the above.
11. Embrace your inner spaz, nerd, geek and freak.

How to be OMFG creative.

1. Live the life you envision in your wildest dreams.
2. Write your Oscar acceptance speech. Win a gold medal. Run for Supreme Alfa Queen Gawddess Bufu of the Universe Galaxy.
3. Be spontaneous! Let go of inhibitions! Play! Be wildly silly and bravely free!
4. Go places you've never been. Do things you've never done. Daily.
5. Make stuff from scratch.
6. Be inventive and original! Make up words, sayings and earth-shattering philosophies! Wear your Clan of the Cave Bear outfit with pride. Dance like a Ninja Hillbilly. Talk like a pirate. Do animal impersonations.
7. Rant and rave about everything.
8. Play different characters or inanimate objects such as a queen, a thief, a circus freak, a lovesick armadillo or a lost paper airplane.
9. Crack open your dark twisty place and let the light in.
10. See words as if they were pictures. Listen to the silence. Touch emotions. Taste the elements and smell colours.
11. Celebrate and covet weirdness

How to surprise people.

1. Perfect the "Art of Scardiation★." Jump out of a closet, bush or shower. Hide a plastic rat in a drawer. Put a fake bug in the bed and other immature and unexpected acts of hilarious trickery.
2. Be spontaneous: celebrate International Donut day.
3. Reveal a hidden talent like being able to tie cherry stems with your tongue. I KNOW! You never would have guessed – thirteen in a row!
4. Speak in Snerney Berney★.
5. Throw a "come as you are surprise party" at someone else's house.
6. Give random gifts of kindness: coffee, flowers, a candy bar, a vacation to Paris or a new hamster.
7. Call someone you haven't spoken to in 10 years.
8. Invite people to your cottage for a clothing optional weekend.
9. Show up at work wearing your mermaid tail.
10. Show off your extra toe, finger or nipple.
11. Admit that you started a Tony Orlando & Dawn fan club.

How to be adventurous.

1. Dare yourself on a daily and hourly basis.
2. Really what do you have to lose? Except everything you have to gain.
3. Consider what being the alternative would be like: boring Betty, Doris dullard, safety Sue or wimpy Wilma. No thanks!
4. Stretch yourself beyond your comfort zone. Try tiger tiger licorice mandarin orange instead of vanilla; wear heliotrope instead of black and talk to strangers instead of friends.
5. Start with an adventurous mind. Visualize the story, the events and the possibilities; build the mental excitement, create desire, passion and wonder. Feels good, right? Now go do it for real!
6. Don't dwell on the negative "what ifs?". What if the volcano erupts? What if I come across a bear? What if the cute guy with the plaid shirt and dimples says he doesn't want to go out with me? What if you rescue a pack of alpacas trying to escape the erupting volcano? What if you share your jar of peanut butter with your newfound friend, Yogi? What if Mr. Lumberjack says, "yes…what took you so long?"
7. Think of the stories you'll be able to tell. For example, the time I was bathing with elephants in Nepal and was thrown off and swallowed infested river water and came down with the plague while hiking the Everest trail, having to excuse myself in the tall grass to sh#t my brains out only to realize my butt was covered in hungry leeches that the guide had to pick off…just as an example.
8. Channel your inner pioneer, daredevil, explorer and high-wire acrobat.
9. Understand that when you take risks or embark on an adventure, you will discover new talents, expand your wisdom, enhance your emotional capacity and really get to know yourself.
10. Take the plunge. Grab the bull by the horns. Ring the bell and for the love of DOG just do it. You won't be sorry - you'll be exhilarated.
11. One life. Once chance to live it.

How to be organized.

1. Make TO DO lists for this minute, hour, day and week. Put your items on your calendar, in your planner and/or Smartphone or colour-coordinated post-it notes. Cross things off as completed (it feels good)!
2. Use file folders. Label the files and put stuff in them. File everything.
3. Alphabetize, categorize, classify and catalogue your records, recipes, receipts and random bits and pieces.
4. Colour coordinate your closet according to articles of clothing and the different seasons.
5. Use boxes, baskets and bins for yarn, buttons, crafts, spices, utensils, apples, toys, magazines, mail and mitts. Get the idea?
6. Stay tidy. Repeat after me: EVERYTHING has its place. Put it there. NOW!
7. Simplify your surroundings. Clear up clutter. Throw shit out. Have a yard sale, donate stuff or give it away. Just get rid of stuff that you don't need.
8. Don't delay, postpone or procrastinate. Do what needs to be done now. Have you done it yet? What are you waiting for? Get on it!
9. Tick tock: wear a watch.
10. Multi-task your responsibilities. Pick up your groceries, dry cleaning, present for Lulu, pet food for Angus and get a pedicure on the way home. Map out your day and your tasks so that you can create a plan of attack.
11. Work on developing some anal-retentive, obsessive-compulsive tendencies. I can help.

How to slow down.

1. Engage the brakes. Get off the train. Hang out at the station.
2. Be the turtle. Be the snail. Be the sloth.
3. Walk, don't run. Chew food, don't inhale it. Contemplate circumstances, don't agitate them.
4. Meditate as if you're sitting in molasses.
5. Learn to breathe and be in the moment.
6. Sit outside. Listen to the wind. Talk to the birds. Watch the bees. Smell the roses.
7. Understand the difference between a leisurely versus a lazy pace.
8. Know that doing nothing is actually doing something.
9. Singletask for a change.
10. Discover the joy of stillness. Schedule one slow hour a day to be still, drift, float, linger and lull in quietude.
11. Give yourself permission to.

How to relax.

1. Take 5 or 10! If you're stressed out mentally or physically stop what you're doing and let it go.
2. Find your bliss. What makes you truly happy? Being outside, reading, cooking or making art? Do that.
3. Go for a soak! Pour yourself a luxurious bubble bath with your rubber ducky and all! Include candles, incense, wine or another person - even more relaxing!
4. Pet your pet. If you don't have a pet, pet yourself. Nudge, nudge, wink, wink!
5. Unplug your phone, computer, TV and any other devices that keep you constantly connected. Free yourself…even if it's just for a while.
6. Hang out in nature. Listen to the birds, breathe in the air and walk barefoot in the grass.
7. Sit in stillness. Breathe deeply. Daydream or meditate.
8. Listen to music. It soothes the savage beast!
9. Bend, stretch and shake out the kinks. Get a massage. Try yoga. Go for a walk, run or bike ride. Get some exercise but make sure it's for pleasure not punishment.
10. Laugh! A good belly laugh lowers your stress hormone levels and raises your endolphins★ which help your mood.
11. Pour yourself a big fat goblet of wine.

How to meditate.

1. Make the choice to be still, especially if the notion of sitting still causes you to vibrate and break out in a rash while blurting Tourette-like obscenities at the ceiling.
2. Get off the train and the hamster wheel. Stop running, doing, thinking. Take a break and invite quiet into your brain and body.
3. Don't do it for Oprah, Deepak, Buddha or Maharishi Mahesh Yogi. Do it for you.
4. Say no to multitasking. No, you can't clean the kitchen and meditate! Resign yourself to doing just one thing. Start with breathing. (I know… stressful!)
5. Set time aside. 20 minutes to meditate…ok start with 10.
6. Lie down. Invite your 15 lb cat to lie on your chest to keep you there.
7. Create a relaxing environment. Dim the lights, put on some monk music, light incense and let the sound of chimes carry you into a blissful state of utopia. Are you floating yet?
8. If that isn't working then visualize butterflies and bunnies playing in your ethereal headspace.
9. Amp it up a notch and add in a mantra. Pick a simple word or phrase, like OM or Fudge, to connect you to the ever-flowing chi that fills each chakra and to open each lotus flower into serene elation. WTF?
10. Redefine your inner Zen – perhaps try envisioning your inner Zebra leaping over fences and frolicking in fields of pop tarts.
11. Trust that you will undergo a phenomenal change where every cell in your body will be filled with more energy. This will result in joy, peace, enthusiasm, easy sleep, a fresh and alert mind, increased creativity, intuition and an expanded consciousness of happiness. Believe me, it's true!

Good to Know

How to buy a home and be a homeowner.

1. Talk to EVERYONE who has already done it. Get recos of good real estate peeps, mortgage brokers, banks and contractors. Find smarty pants math friends who excel at budget spreadsheets and get them to hold your hand throughout the entire process because it can be a really grown-up thing to do!
2. Research what to look for when checking out your potential new dream home. Check out the pipes, wires, foundation, leaky basements, termites, neighbours and ghost busters.
3. Say hello to pinching pennies! Say hello to a super smart and financially grown-up investment in your future.
4. Hide several sets of keys outside because you will lock yourself out - like I did the first morning I got possession. I woke up at the crack of dawn to unpack and went out onto the porch for just a second to grab my first mail. The door slammed shut. I was locked out wearing nothing - and I mean nothing - but a dirty old wife beater tank top. It was 5am, I was mostly naked and I had no phone. I hailed a teenaged boy going by on his bike. He climbed up my drainpipe, broke into the second floor bedroom window and let me in. So hide your extra set of keys. And wear pj bottoms.
5. Create your new world! It's your love shack, castle, palace, pad, abode and sanctuary to do whatever you want with! Paint the walls orange and fuchsia, get that fun fur sofa, put art on the ceilings, design your theme rooms and of course plant poppies and put ceramic squirrels on the front lawn!
6. Learn to DIY. Buy tools and learn how to use them. Pull up carpets, strip wallpaper, paint every room a different colour, caulk the tub, plant a wild flower garden and refinish furniture that you found in the trash. Home Depot will become your new best friend.
7. Accept that you will become your parents. Buy a toilet plunger. Buy a snow shovel. Cut the grass, put out the trash, turn off the lights, lower the heat and don't waste water…it costs money, you know!
8. Prepare for disasters – like amorous raccoons who move in underneath your sunroom and make mad passionate raccoon love for months and then produce nests of babies that require them to stay until they are old enough to climb out and be safely trapped (unharmed) and released far away at a cost of $700.

9. Or you may encounter weepy basement walls that sprout holes when the monsoon season hits that causes a basement flood, complete with floating cardboard boxes and kittens learning the back stroke. And the power may be out so it's pitch black and you can't find the emergency flashlight and the shop wet vac won't work. And it happens every time it rains, so you suck it up and buy a sump pump for the low, low price of $6000. I named her Shirley and it's been dry ever since!
10. Or what about an ice storm that brings $1000 worth of trees smashing down in the backyard crushing all the power lines and cutting power, heat and water to the house for 6 days? I had to pee into a bucket and tuck my 3 cats and myself into my -40F sub-Arctic sleeping bag.
11. On a happier note…celebrate! You are also now THE PARTY HOUSE! Gather your gang, hang out, host awesome dance nights, potlucks, dips & sips and backyard bashes!

How to be crafty (in a good way).

1. See beauty in everything.
2. Collect junk, scraps of fabric, yarn, paper, rocks and wood, broken bits of china, glass, toys and trinkets. It will all come in handy one day!
3. Make things from scratch like lampshades, bubble bath and brownies.
4. Seize the opportunity to be original and start a new trend. For instance, you can create critter costumes for hamsters.
5. Pick up an "old school is cool" hobby like sewing, knitting, embroidery, quilting, candle-making, macramé and popsicle placemats.
6. Don't try to be Martha Stewart. Create your own crafty cup of tea and own it.
7. Release your inner child artist. Grab a glue stick, put your fingers in paint, make a mess and call it art!
8. Find crafty treasures in unlikely places such as yard sales, Goodwill and the trash bin.
9. Be an artistic environmentalist! From fashion to furniture - re-purpose, re-vitalize, re-finish, re-love.
10. Discover the Zen of crafting – set-up a seraphic zone of absolute utter creative bliss.
11. Express your emotions visually.

How to throw an awesome party.

1. Invite awesome people.
2. Dress code 101. Encourage ensembles that embrace everything from flamboyant and frilly to casual and comfy – whatever rocks your guest's world and wardrobe.
3. Bring out the booze…and lots of it. Always have a "just in case" case of wine on hand.
4. Dish out the grub…and lots of it. From a junk food smorgasbord featuring chips, cheesies, Fritos, Doritos, Hickory sticks, jelly beans, jujubes, gummy worms, licorice and marshmallow everything; to a table of tapas with cheese, crackers, dips, salsa, veggies, olives, appetizers, hors d'oeuvres and delicious little nibbly bits.
5. Always serve dessert: cake, cookies and magic brownies.
6. Did someone say THEME PARTY?! Let your imagination go wild! How about come as you are…or come as your favourite animal, Pyjama Party, Circus Freaks, Beach Party Bingo, Monster Mash, Western, Oscars, Disco, Casino. Just let me wear a costume please!
7. Crank the tunes! Turn up the turntable! Blast from the past and present including: "Staying Alive", "Billy Jean", "Walk this Way" and don't forget "Shake it Off"!
8. Have a DANCE CONTEST! Move the furniture, pull back the rug and make space for some serious boogie down to the disco beat baby!
9. Play GAMES! Pull out the board games, pin the tail on the donkey, Twister, Truth or Dare and my personal favourite, Spin the Bottle.
10. Give out loot bags. Duh.
11. Make the breakfast of champions – greasy eggers, sausages and a bit of the hair of the dog that bit ya – for the crashers.

How to be a pet owner.

1. Prepare to hand over your heart.
2. Consider the decision to have a pet to be as important as having a kid. It's a huge responsibility and joy. Are you willing and able to walk your St. Bernard named Tiny twice daily? If not then perhaps watching Goldie swim circles is a better place to start. Or a pet rock.
3. What kind of breed of fluffy should you get? Do you want a dog, cat, bird, bunny, hamster, horse, fish, ferret, reptile or tarantula? Consider the factors of temperament (dwarf hamsters are bossy, but teddy bear hamsters are just that), size (Great Dane or Chihuahua) and shedding potential (lizards don't but bunnies…ever hear of dust bunnies?)
4. Learn animal speak. Master the sounds of the gulp, meow, ruff, squeak, snort and similar high pitched boogie woogie, snerney berney, little muffinball, poohead, kitten bum-bum and other verbal nonsense of pure loviation.
5. Poo happens. So does pee, barf and hacked-up furballs. Usually it happens in your favourite shoes, on your pillow and definitely on expensive Moroccan carpets.
6. Just like humans, every animal has its own personality. They have their likes, dislikes, neuroses, voice, fave toy, outfit, place to hide, sleep, eat and way to show affection. Angus sucks earlobes, Pagan shows you his belly and Fiend likes to stick her tongue in my nostril. Awe!
7. You can spend 100s of dollars on toys, but your pet will always think that the best ones are your slippers, tissue paper, toilet paper rolls and cardboard boxes.
8. Consider the fact that your home is now their home. Dogs require a safe, fenced-in yard. Cats need scratching posts or your favourite velvet armchair. Bunnies can be trained to run free but copper-cover all cords and hamsters really appreciate the intergalactic adventures of The Super Hammy Space Habitat complete with the revolving spaceship.

9. Prepare to spend some serious coin. Vet bills suck. Winston, my dwarf hamster, got a peanut wedged in his cheek. It got moldy, turned into an abscess and infected his tooth. It was a $200 surgery bill to remove it. A $6 hamster with a $200 dental bill. Ouch!
10. Congrats! You now have a new best friend who will love you, listen to you, be there for you, lick your tears, play with you, keep you company, make you laugh and love you like never before.
11. "Until one has loved an animal, a part of one's soul remains unawakened." *Anatole France*

How to be eco-friendly.

1. Treat Mother Nature like you would treat your own Mother – with respect, care and love.
2. One person's junk is another one's treasure. See beauty in the broken and cast out items. Cruise the curb for fabulous finds like furniture, frames and miscellaneous fixings that may just need a little finessing and finishing up.
3. Love the pre-loved. Shop at thrift stores, Goodwill and yard sales.
4. Re-cycle. Not just the typical plastic, paper and bottles, but larger items like electronics, tires and mattresses. Also consider re-using items like jars, plastic bags, boxes, wood, rocks and fabric.
5. Be doubly thoughtful when giving a gift. Spare don't tear and re-gift the wrap. Also present your present with re-useable items such as tea towels, bandanas or homemade, hand-painted brown paper bags. And you can always re-gift a gift that you never really liked!
6. Get crafty! Old jewellery, forks, spoons and hangers make for a pretty musical chime. Bricks or pieces of wood make for a great garden path. Holey socks make great sock monkeys.
7. Re- fashion. Take that boring navy blazer and swap in some fun fur cuffs, add a little polka dot ruffle around the edges and voila! Before you toss out your gold lamé jumpsuit, consider keeping the love going by gathering your pals for a clothing swap. Scraps of fabric come in handy for mending holes in jeans; old curtains make great pillows or placemats.
8. Donate everything from clothing, furniture, books, records, toys, computers, eyeglasses and sporting goods. Share the love.
9. Conserve water. Collect an outdoor water barrel or better yet, share a shower!
10. Turn off the lights and enjoy the candlelight.
11. Go wild! Plant trees. Grow plants that attract bees and butterflies. Have a birdfeeder, a squirrel feeder and a bat box.

Love

How to love yourself.

1. Choose to love yourself. You are loveable.
2. Be brave. Open your heart. Remove your armor - let your love light shine.
3. Accept and cherish yourself for who you really are, not who people think you should be.
4. Understand the difference between being narcissistic, conceited, selfish and self-serving. Put yourself first!
5. Give yourself 5 compliments a day. Awesome sauce curls, Patty!
6. Give yourself what you need: space, time, quiet, respect, marshmallows or wine.
7. Decipher what the hardest things to love about yourself are. Is it your body, curly hair, attitude, morals or moles? Then fall madly and passionately in love with those aspects of you. Be swoon worthy!
8. Treat yourself the same way as someone you love.
9. Develop a crush on you. Stroke your ego. Romance your reflection. Date your psyche. Care for your body. Hug your heart.
10. Spend time with yourself. Take yourself on a date. Pamper yourself. Rendezvous with you!
11. Love what is unique about you. Remember they broke the mould; you are one-of-a-kind, rare and an original.

How to fall in love.

1. Remove the chains around your heart.
2. Reap what you sow. Plant the seeds of possibility.
3. Own your "loveableness".
4. Call off the dragons. Lower the drawbridge. Share the key to the castle and crack open the vault.
5. Don't define it. Just enjoy it. Just be love, don't need to have to fall into it.
6. If you want love, you must give love.
7. Find the right person. Being compatible matters! For example, if he loves pickles and you hate pickles then he gets all the pickles!
8. No one is perfect. Love means finding their idiosyncrasies charming, like his adorable guttural snore.
9. Build trust. Be honest. Be real. Be you.
10. Really appreciate the other person.
11. Throw away the rulebook. There are no instructions other than following your heart.

How to find true love.

1. Start with loving yourself. And I mean that in more ways than one.
2. Give love without expectations.
3. Think about what love means to you. Never settle.
4. Don't have a must-have list. Be open to surprises.
5. Instead of saying that you're lonely, say that you are loveable.
6. Wander the aisles of Home Depot and ask men about screwdrivers or offer up zucchini recipes in the veggie department.
7. Smile, sparkle, wink, flirt, bat your come-hither eyelashes; remember that you're irresistible.
8. Leave your couch. Go online. Go on coffee dates. Leave your house. Banter with boys at the bus stop. Gather your gals and grab a drink at a bar, attend an event or a concert. Volunteer, join a club or ride your bike and crash into the cutie. Oops. Blink, blink. If there's a will, there's a way.
9. Apparently, blah, blah, blah, "he'll show up when you least expect it". So go on, head outside in your dirty track pants with no make-up on, greasy hair in a bun, sans underwear and he'll be buying chips at your local C-store. Swoon!
10. Fire up the Gawddess and cast a love spell…eye of newt, cinnamon, vanilla and whisky…and that's just behind your ears.
11. MANifest. Wink, wink.

How to flirt.

1. Learn from the best – Suzanne Fleishman, 1989.
2. Subtlety is key. Having your boobs hanging out, thong string showing or wearing a micro-miniscopic skirt is way too overt.
3. Engage your imagination! Think flirty thoughts. Daydream about dreamy rendezvous. Covet kisses.
4. It's all in the eyes: slow, deliberate, focused and come-hither smize. Blink, blink.
5. Wear rosewood, vanilla or whisky behind the ears and knees.
6. Enjoy oysters, chocolate, honey, figs and yes, asparagus. You are what you eat.
7. Be playful. Coquettishly tease. Be the kitten hiding the tiger. Leave them wanting more.
8. Be confident with your body language. Be open (uncross your arms), initiate contact, "accidently" brush-up beside them and let your finger touch their forearm, their lip.
9. Be playful with sexual innuendos. Aim for total innocence but deliver the goods.
10. Sweet talk with compliments, humour and nicknames (when spoken in a whisper it works wonders).
11. Be bold. Make the first move. Take the bull by the balls…er…horns.

How to feel sexy.

1. Own your awesomeness. Whether you're wearing stilettos or sneakers, silk or flannel, jeans or a little black dress, it's how you feel not how you look.
2. Engage your inner Gawddess, diva, dame, siren and sex kitten.
3. Develop an appetite. Turn up the heat and start cooking. Whip up a tempting dish with a little spice, sauciness and sizzle.
4. Speak in a whisper.
5. Use your mouth. Share some serious lip service. Divulge wanton words with a libidinous tone. They don't call it intercourse for nothing.
6. Be playful like a chipmunk.
7. Wear fancy panties. Take them or leave them…off.
8. Body language 101: flirt with your smile. Taunt with your hands. Seduce with your eyes.
9. Be natural. Sexy is in your nature.
10. Confidence is irresistible.
11. Take control.

Nature

How to be one with nature.

1. Embrace the elements. Gather freckles from the sunshine. Find your fins in the water. Wave your wings in the air and fly, fuel your spirit from the fire and ignite it.
2. Learn to speak chipmunk, squirrel, bunny, groundhog, porcupine, deer, fox, wolf, bear and forest zombie.
3. Understand that the only thing that deters mosquitoes or black flies is to drink whisky.
4. Outdoor must-have emergency supplies: pocket knife, compass, matches, whistle, water bottle, junk food and booze.
5. Outhouse/bush can etiquette 101: always bring TP and matches to burn TP, wet ones for wipes and don't forget to check for spiders, slugs and leeches before squatting.
6. Get to know Mother Nature, the Green man, water nymphs, Naiads, Sylphs, Elves, Wood Sprites, Gnomes, Fauns and of course, Faeries – they will protect and be with you forever.
7. Bon fire rituals: roasted marshmallow Smores, star gazing, sing-songing, drumming, guitaring, telling ghost stories and the infamous "scary walk" to the abandoned cemetery down the road without a flashlight.
8. Hug a tree, roll in the dirt, skinny dip, find faces in clouds, listen to the wind speak, bathe in the rapids, watch a spider spin a web, feed chipmunks, tame a little red squirrel, befriend a blue jay, hunt for mushrooms, play hide & go seek in the forest, stoke a bonfire, catch fireflies, bang a drum, strum a guitar and sip some sauce under the stars.
9. Be bear friendly – always make noise when walking through the woods so you don't scare a bear. If you come across one, lower your eyes (do not wink) and slowly back away. If the bear snorts, become as big as you can to scare him (good luck with that). If he starts to growl, hit the ground and cover your head (they tend to go for the neck and limbs first) or for the love of yogi just give him your jar of peanut butter.
10. Wilderness isn't just a place it's a state of being.
11. G.O.D. Great. Out. Doors.

How to communicate with animals, bugs and birds.

1. Always introduce yourself. "Hi perfect little creature of the universe, I'm Patty – animal lover and whisperer of all things furry, fluttery and freaky looking." See they've also been told not to speak to strangers…so don't be one.
2. Make eye contact. Wink.
3. Let them sniff you. Return the courtesy.
4. Feel their heartbeat. Get in sync with their body language. Breathe together. Earn trust. Respect their existence and then coexist.
5. Speak in a soft and squeaky manner. International animal speak is at least five decibels higher than a normal human voice and has much more dramatic inflections.
6. Revel in rhyme. For example, "Awe, boogie woogie, snerney berney, poodie moodie, shoodie."
7. Give them the space to respond. They may have their own unique way. Be patient and be open to it. They may place a paw on your foot, tilt their head, land on your shoulder, buzz in your ear or my personal favourite, suck your earlobe (I love you too Angus).
8. Pay attention to their voices. Listen to the variations in squeaks, meows, purrs, growls, squawks, screeches, buzzes, barks, twitters, tweets, whistles, chirps, shrills, snorts, hoots, howls, yelps, clicks, caws, coos, whoops and eeks. They all tell a different story.
9. Name every critter and creature you meet. It makes them feel familiar and loved. Nick the chipmunk, Henry the jay, Ruby the hummingbird, Lucy the spider. Besides it's nice to be on a first name basis.
10. Talk about things that interest them. For instance, chipmunks love to discuss the difference between salted and regular peanuts and the eternal contest to see how many nuts they can shove in their cheeks. Random dogs on the street love to be asked if they are the cutest puppy ever. Squirrels love to brag about their playful climbing prowess and spiders just want to be told that they are pretty.
11. Treat animals as you would want them to treat you, but consider holding off on the licking part.

How to travel off the beaten path.

1. Forget about everything you know or have been warned about.
2. Talk to strangers…the stranger the better!
3. Pet stray animals, nuzzle noses with rhinos, take a bath with an elephant and most of all hug every monkey you come across.
4. Make friends with the locals – they'll take you to the coolest nooks and crannies, get you dancing with the tribe and make you part of their family forever.
5. Eat everything you can't pronounce or recognize even if it has more than 4 legs.
6. Get up at 5am to see a local market come alive.
7. Learn how to say hello and thank you in the local language.
8. Perfect your squat. BYOTP (toilet paper).
9. Practice the philosophy of "when in Rome."
10. Embrace every breath, hiccup, bump or bombshell as an adventure – adventures make the best stories once you return home.
11. Be the path. Put on your Dora the Explorer hat, relinquish the itinerary and embark on an adventure yet to be defined.

Stressy Stuff

Fear

How to break through insurmountable fear.

1. Lose the crutch.
2. Feel everything and revel in it. (F.E.A.R.)
3. Know that fearing something is way worse than facing it. And by not facing it you are choosing to hold onto it.
4. Get some perspective on the situation. Compare it to being eaten by a bear…one limb at a time.
5. Don't anticipate a herd of rhinos coming when it's probably just a box of kittens.
6. Have an escape plan or two in your back pocket.
7. Shine up your shield. Call on your super powers. Put up your sword and slay the dragon.
8. Conjure up the magic. Manifest a spell. Create your own abracadabra. Believe you can and will do it.
9. Don't start with a marathon…begin with baby steps.
10. Take a deep breath and…push send, ask him/her out, ask for help, stand up for yourself, say no, say yes, embrace discomfort, embody hope or invite change.
11. Trust that you will probably, most certainly survive and be stronger, smarter and braver. And you will have earned the cape!

How to manage unreasonable stress.

1. Separate it into buckets so that it isn't overwhelming and you can tackle it in chunks. For example: impending apocalypses, work, money, family, health and STUPID BOYS.
2. Get it out of your head. Put it on paper. Write a letter. Write a list of pros and cons, what to do/not to do, best and worst case scenarios and fantasy versus reality scenarios. Express your feelings, tell it like it is, rant, rave, ridicule and release. Then post it, hide it or burn it.
3. Eat chips. Drink wine. Repeat.
4. Exercise. Walk to the corner store to buy more chips. Put them on the top shelf so that you have to move a chair and get up and down to get them.
5. Obsessively clean your house. Empty your closets. Throw out useless shit. Organize your drawers. Colour-coordinate your socks and underwear. Alphabetize your records. Wash your floor (so when you're lying on it in a fetal position, at least it's clean).
6. Get everyone's opinion as to what to do – but don't follow any of it. Trust your gut. Even if you need to make a mistake – it's yours and it will be your lesson to learn.
7. Apparently, breathing helps. Slow, deep, repetitive belly breaths are good. Just don't hyperventilate and pass out.
8. Do something nice for yourself. Eat Mac & Cheese, take a lavender bubble bath, buy fabric or hire a hitman.
9. Rip something up. Stomp your feet. Throw an axe.
10. Start fresh every day.
11. Believe that no matter what – you will be just fine. Because you already are!

How to cope with anxiety.

1. Know that you are not alone. It may feel like you are, but you are not alone.
2. Reach out for help. Call upon friends, family, therapists, doctors, your pets and invisible imaginary friends (just because you can't see them doesn't mean that they aren't able to hear you).
3. Medicate. Plain and simple, your mind is not your own. It's been abducted by the most terrifying of unrealities, pain and despair. Whether you choose natural or pharma, it really does help reconfigure your marbles so that you can at least start to use your brain again. AND THERE IS NO SHAME IN TAKING MEDICATION.
4. Apply the magic of nature's natural remedies: chamomile tea, Bach's Rescue Remedy, lavender oil, lemon balm or my favourite…"a forest bath"…20 minutes in the woods, inhaling the woodsy earth and listening to the whispering trees. See! You're already feeling calmer!
5. Understand that an anxiety attack is a mind state that manifests in a physical reaction. They may be scary as all hell but usually there is no real danger. Stop catastrophizing! Close your eyes, breathe and rationalize your thoughts. It's not a Zombie Apocalypse…it's more likely a box of kittens.
6. Open wide and take huge, deep, slow breaths. Then focus on one tiny, simple happy place, visual or word to bring you back. I find sparkly unicorns playing in fields of rainbow daisies particularly good.
7. Move. Change your scene. Get out of bed. Get off the floor. Take a baby step. Being paralyzed contains the fear…even a little motion helps to defuse the adrenaline of fight or flight.
8. Collect coping techniques. Write down what you are feeling (get it out). Create calm by listening to music or meditation tapes. Create order by tidying your space or organizing some drawers. Distract yourself with a relaxing hobby. Sing a song, it helps you breathe and distracts you from the panic.
9. Face what scares you. WTF? Ya, it sound tough, but it's true. Hiding from it doesn't make it go away. Slay the dragon or make friends with him.
10. Recognize your triggers. Get rid of them, avoid them and protect yourself against them.
11. Trust that you can and will get through it. Give yourself time.

How to have faith in the unknown.

1. Think of it as simply unfamiliar, untold, unspoken, unrealized…a mystery yet to be revealed.
2. For sure science, research and evolution make a lot of sense, but so does fate, kismet, destiny and miracles.
3. Treat the unknown like a stranger who's going to be your new best friend – but you just haven't met him or her yet.
4. Think back to all of your previous unknowns like your first job, first kiss, first home hair dye job or even when you tasted a pickle for the first time. See? You survived it (barely).
5. Change the phrase "fear of the unknown" to "beer of the unknown". Who doesn't want to try a new beer?
6. Ask yourself what's behind curtain #2 – a fire-breathing dragon or a kitten? Assume that the unknown is something good.
7. A great antidote to not knowing how something is going to turn out is to trust thy gut. Sure it may be tricky to trust others or a new environment or what your lifeline is going to be. But you can trust yourself and choose to make the most of it no matter what.
8. Embrace the element of surprise, the mystic of mystery, the climax of a good cliff-hanger.
9. Marry the notion of unknown to adventure.
10. Focus on the "know" part of unknown.
11. Be live. Believe.

How to manage a bad case of the nerves.

1. Close your eyes…maybe it will disappear.
2. Breathe. Five, deep, slow, belly-filling breaths. Do it again. Try not to hyperventilate.
3. Get up, go for a walk or do the hokey-pokey. Shake it off.
4. Get perspective. Reason with yourself and the situation. Weigh the possibilities against the probabilities.
5. Sneak a peek into the worst case scenario (alien invasion) and realize that regardless of what happens you will survive…and if you don't then there's nothing to worry about.
6. Grab hold of Rescue Remedy or whisky…whatever's closest at hand.
7. Meditate. Centre yourself. Focus on breathing. Be the tree…be the tree… be the fucking tree…or just cut it down.
8. Get it out of your system. Hide in the bathroom and have a good cry, rant to a friend, co-worker and random stranger on the bus…just don't let it fester.
9. Apply positive affirmations. Tell yourself that you can do this! Tell yourself that you are brave! Tell yourself that you are awesome and gosh darn it – people love you!
10. Distract yourself. Go watch a cute animal video. I find goats particularly calming.
11. If all else fails, remember that whatever doesn't kill ya makes you stronger.

How to let go of worry.

1. Ask yourself what purpose does worrying serve (other than to give you wrinkles!).
2. Ask yourself if your worry is real or imagined. Are you being rational? Are you in control of the outcome, the solution? Is there anything you can do to remedy the situation?
3. Until you know the outcome anticipate the arrival of a box of kittens instead of a herd of rhinos.
4. Wait until "what if" and "worst case scenarios" are your actual reality. Until the end of the world comes assume that it will be the best-case scenario.
5. Distract yourself. Watch TV, listen to music, go to a movie, go for a walk, exercise, cook, make art and make love.
6. Take deep breaths. Grab some Rescue Remedy. Get fresh air. Take a shot of whisky. Talk to a friend or your pet.
7. Stay in the NOW. Live one moment at a time.
8. Consider the theory that "what you think, you create". Friendly monsters! Think positive thoughts.
9. Trick your mind with a visual or phrase. For example, every time your worry enters your mind, picture a rainbow elephant and pay complete attention to that rainbow elephant for as long as possible. OR create a mantra like "Love the shit outta everything" that breaks your worry train of thought.
10. Come up with an escape plan…just in case.
11. Trust that you can handle anything because you can.

Inner Strength

How to cope with being broken.

1. If at first duct tape doesn't work try something a little stronger…like therapy.
2. Don't rush to run the marathon when what you really need is to figure out your first step.
3. Accept your break. Whether it be a bone, a relationship, a job or an outlook on life – you broke for a reason and it will present an incredible opportunity to learn invaluable things about yourself…like patience, vulnerability, strength, hope, humour, empathy and new beginnings.
4. Crutches may assist a broken leg, but they do nothing for a broken spirit. Ditch them. You may stumble and fall but you will learn how to get up without them.
5. Invisible breaks like your heart, mind or spirit are much harder to fix and require a much longer, gentler approach to heal…sometimes years.
6. Being broken is painful both mentally and physically. Sometimes a pill can help; other times physiotherapy can help. And sometimes nothing helps – other than allowing yourself to feel the pain in all its horror and then release it in order to deal with it and ultimately heal.
7. Sticks & stones may break your bones, so does tobogganing, falling off tables, down stairs, getting hit by a bus and slipping onto a spiky bedpost. I've broken my legs, fingers, toes, hands, feet, collarbone, cheekbone and back; bodies are amazingly resilient and if you take good care of them, you can bounce back with a wicked cartwheel. I'm living proof.
8. Be vulnerable. Ask for help. Accept it. You don't have to be invincible because - FYI – you're not.
9. Call upon the power of attitude and choice to help navigate your path. Trust me I know how hard this can be, but it's honestly half the battle. Your thoughts, feelings and beliefs make a huge difference in how well your healing process will go. Choose hope, positivity and decide to never give up.
10. Get creative with things like stairs, grocery shopping, getting dressed, having a bath, filling the cats' water bowls and uncorking a bottle of wine. These are HUGE challenges with broken bits and pieces. You won't believe how imaginative you will become. Mantra – where there is a will there is a way.
11. Give yourself a break. Have patience little grasshopper…time heals everything.

How to cope when you're not.

1. Time to earn that Oscar. Call upon your best Meryl Streep or Daniel Day Lewis impression.
2. If you are going to spontaneously combust into hysterical tears or a murderous rant – find a bathroom, boardroom or closet and let it rip in private.
3. Go shopping. Treat yourself to bad girl comfort food. Go for a walk. Have a bath. Talk to a squirrel. Just go do something other than fret.
4. Talk to yourself (like you don't already!). Tell yourself that you are amazing and strong and people like you gosh darn it all. Because they do. And post post-it notes with reminders of that too.
5. Lay on your kitchen floor in a fetal position. The cool tiles will help snap you back into reality if the filthy under the fridge crumbs don't completely gross you out of your boo hoo mood.
6. Pray or just talk to the ceiling. Tell your pets the whole story. Call a friend even if all you can do is breathe. Meditate. Medicate. Hallucinate. Escape the vortex of this moment and shift to another…even if only for a moment and the next and the next.
7. Don't rush the stages. Don't deny that you're in denial. Go ahead and be fricking fracking angry. Make a deal, bargain and always take door #3. You've got to feel it to heal it. It's ok to feel sad, lost, alone, scared and helpless – just know it is temporary. And trust that finally the day will come where you don't hurt anymore and you can rip off the Flintstone Band-Aid.
8. Read "Oh the places you will go" by Dr. Seuss. He's a doctor after all.
9. Engage your superpowers. Put on your peril sensitive glasses. Activate the cone of silence and be prepared to beam me up Scotty.
10. Allow the "big girl" you to tell the "little girl" you that everything is going to be ok.
11. Believe all Momisms: "This too shall pass." "Take one day at a time." "Tomorrow is another day." "Life isn't fair." And "you'll understand when you're older."

How to keep yourself motivated.

1. Be hungry for more. Want it. Need it. Covet it. Go get it.
2. Give yourself gold stars. Create a chart and reward yourself so that you can highlight your progress! You can also use unicorn or kitty stickers if you want.
3. Be accountable. Commit publicly! Tell everyone what your goal is. Have an accountability buddy to check-in with.
4. Adopt affirmations like "YOU CAN DO IT.", "EAT FEAR FOR BREAKFAST." or "LOVE THE SHIT OUTTA EVERYTHING."
5. Have a theme song like "Shake it Off" by Taylor Swift.
6. Take baby steps. Start small – don't over extend yourself. Run your own race then work your way up to the marathon. Build on your successes.
7. Just do it. Suck it up chicken butt…stop with the excuses! You are in charge of you.
8. Jump off the failure ferris wheel and jump back on the winner's wagon.
9. Find your inspiration. Are you saving for a trip? Post pictures of your dream adventure. Trying to lose weight? Put the scale in front of the fridge or hang your bikini in plain sight.
10. Focus on the benefits, not the challenge.
11. Claim your cause, desire a dream and grab onto your greater purpose.

How to trust and be trusted.

1. Understand first and foremost that trust is earned.
2. Ask important questions then repeat them to see if you get the same answers. Have you ever been to jail? Do you have a girlfriend?
3. Listen carefully. Don't hear what you want to hear.
4. If you build it, it will come.
5. Be reliable and expect the same of others.
6. Your word means everything.
7. Give the benefit of the doubt once.
8. Always tell the truth…it's easier to remember.
9. Go with your gut…its right 99% of the time.
10. Consider trustworthiness to be the most fragile, valuable and irreplaceable quality that you possess – protect and cherish it.
11. Cross your heart, hope to die and stick a needle in your eye.

How to forgive.

1. Life is hard. Shit happens, hurtful shit. Ask yourself if you are going to let this take over your life and define you.
2. Equate blame with self-inflicted poison.
3. Revenge may seem wonderfully satisfying but remember the sayings: an eye for an eye and two wrongs don't make a right.
4. Be the better person. Even if it's just for a few minutes, take a walk in the other person's shoes. Try on their perspective, their actions and their regret or ignorance.
5. Find the silver lining. Look at it as a life lesson and required learning.
6. Holy heavy negativity! Relinquish the weight. You can't control or change what has happened, but you can control and change how you choose to deal with it. Set yourself free.
7. Consider the notions of blame, fault, right versus wrong and the assignment of responsibility. Then consider the notions of compassion, mercy, reconciliation and grace.
8. Realize the hatred or anger that you feel is invisible to your adversary and is only hurting you.
9. Mistakes – I've made a few as Frank Sinatra says and so has every other living soul on the planet! Hello…human. No one is perfect. Second chances are just that.
10. Know that it takes less energy to love and to forgive than it does to hold a grudge.
11. Wish your enemy well. Kill them with kindness. It will drive them to the brink of insanity and make the Karma Gawds shine on you.

How to let go.

1. Talk it out. Scream it out. Stomp it out. Cry it out. Wish it out. Beg it out. Think it out. Feel it out.
2. Hold on really, really, really tight – so tight that it actually hurts and you simply have to let it go in order to stop the pain.
3. Ask yourself if holding on is working for you? Are they wasting their time thinking, hating, worrying and obsessing about you? I bet you they're not.
4. Sit in a river. Let it carry the weight away. (A bath will do in the absence of a river.)
5. Crank The Bee Gees Greatest Hits (or whatever your go-to tune is) and shake your booty like a wild turkey tornado until all unwanted energy evaporates into bliss-filled molecules of dance.
6. Apparently…stilling the mind works wonders. Apparently this is accomplished by sitting…still…breathing in and out…focusing only on your breath in a peaceful state of OM and nothing else. Good luck with that.
7. Apparently being busy helps keep your mind preoccupied. Begin with re-organizing all your drawers, closets, cupboards and fridge, alphabetizing your record collection (yes I said records), re-painting your entire house, re-landscaping your yard, perfecting your crème brulée recipe or teaching your pets sign language.
8. Train your brain. Reward it with chips when it's good. Spank it when it's bad and thinks negative, hurtful and sad thoughts. Seriously, it's a matter of mind over matter. Did I just say that?
9. Practice. Nip it in the bud. Pull the plug. Grind to a halt. Catch yourself and stop it before the hamster wheel runs rampant and out of control.
10. Write a "see you later, so long you suck, no thanks, don't show your face around here anymore please, Adios, Hasta la vista, Sayonara, bye bye" letter to your negative thoughts then sign it, crumple it up and toss it in the trash.
11. Make peace.

How to stand up for yourself.

1. Get out of your seat. It's time to earn your "no guts, no glory badge".
2. Remember that you matter. A lot.
3. Repeat after me: I am not a victim, shrinking violet or dishrag. I am assertive, authentic and awesome. Having confidence in yourself is the key.
4. Who else do you think is going to do it for you? Put your sword up and your armor on. This is your life, your dragon to slay and your battle to win.
5. Weigh the pros and cons. Is it better to let it fester, poison, pollute and eat away at your self-esteem or to address it, express it and release it? Choose empowerment.
6. Wait until you are in a calm state. There is no need to go Evil-Knievel. Prepare your Oscar nominated speech, memorize it, speak with authority, be prepared for questions and answers and the paparazzi.
7. Know when to be a duck, when to be a dragon and when to be a dove.
8. Don't expect any action. Just do it to be heard.
9. Refrain from using gorilla tactics…pounding your chest, growling and screaming. Instead embrace the poetry of quiet strength.
10. Be vulnerable. Be open. Be honest. Be brave. Be proud of yourself. Go on - you deserve a latté and cookie!
11. Remember at the very least, you must harbour self-worth and self-respect.

How to disarm insecurity.

1. Don't avoid or deny icky situations. Dig deep, tear off the Band-Aid and remove the thorn; it will hurt a lot less once you let it breathe and heal.
2. Own it and turn it into your super power. I call myself the Super Silly-Speller and Grammatically Gaffe Artist Extraordinaire…just as an example!
3. List your accomplishments starting with your Brownie badges.
4. Change "can't" to "can", "won't" to "will" and "no, I'm not", to "yes, I am."
5. Take baby steps. Lose the heels and start off bare foot. See? You didn't fall.
6. Feed yourself compliments, affirmations, high fives and chips every day.
7. Dare to prove yourself wrong. Then give yourself 5 bucks each time you do it. Before you know it you will have money in your bank and feel more financially secure.
8. Ask for feedback. Am I stupid? Do you think I'm crazy? Are my knees too fat? 10 to 1, you're way better off than you think.
9. Connect with a "pump me up" partner in crime. Swap security salutations daily. "Your knees look super slim today!"
10. Get some perspective. Seriously, are you walking a tightrope blindfolded over Niagara Falls? Brushing a tiger's teeth? Betting your life savings in a back alley craps game? Dancing naked in public? Then just go for it! What's the worst that could happen?
11. Pull a Sally Field. You like me, you really, really like me!

How to be honest with yourself.

1. Stop making excuses. Face the facts and stop fooling yourself – you know the truth. Ice cream is not the healthiest source of calcium, veggie chips are not vegetables and just because you can fit into your stretchy, drawstring, oversized track pants doesn't mean you haven't gained weight.
2. Just because you bury it in a rusty chest under lock and key and hide it under the stairs in the haunted basement with seven boxes on top of it doesn't mean it's not there.
3. Consider just how heavy that falsehood, fib, or fallacy is to carry around every day. Get real. Let it go.
4. Figure out why you think it's better to masquerade, make-believe and pretend? What or whom are you hiding from?
5. Consider the ramifications of being caught in a lie…because one day you will be.
6. Understand the difference between being a great storyteller, yarn spinner and excited embellisher and a full on fake and fraud.
7. There's a great song line in Ricky Nelson's Garden Party…"ya can't please everybody, so ya got to please yourself". Learn it by heart then cross your heart, hope to die and stick a needle in your eye…if you ever forget it.
8. Trust your gut. If the shoe doesn't fit, for the love of Gawd stop wearing it.
9. Come clean. Spill the beans. Fact is better than fiction. The truth will set you free.
10. Ask yourself how reality feels? If it feels natural, effortless and free then foster it. If it sometimes feels scary then that can be your honest place. Stay there and get friendly with it; take care of it and make it feel at home.
11. Ponder the notion of integrity. Who do you want to be? An imposter or the true you?

Sadness

How to cope with regret.

1. Learn from it. It will be your best lesson ever.
2. Ponder the notion that everything happens for a reason.
3. Stop dwelling in shoulda, coulda, woulda land and accept what happened. Take note and don't do it again.
4. Consider whether it was a wrongdoing, an incapability or simply the right choice for you at the time.
5. Ask yourself if there is anything you can do about it. If you can, then do it.
6. Was it something you said, did or didn't do? Determine what you really regret. This will help you sort out your feelings.
7. Make amends. Even if it seems impossible, make amends.
8. Ask for forgiveness.
9. Grieve. Feel sad, guilty, disappointed, confused…then let it go…but never forget it.
10. Acknowledge that life is complex. No one is perfect. Extreme circumstances often instigate extreme actions.
11. Don't look back. Look forward.

How to not feel lonely.

1. Find the comfy place between alone and lonely.
2. Take this time to get to know yourself. Ask yourself questions, ponder your possibilities, make yourself a nice dinner, splash in the bath, buy yourself a present or even take yourself out on a date. Be your own best friend…because btw: YOU ROCK!
3. Whack down the wallows! Get busy. Paint a room, sew a coat, play guitar, re-do your bulletin board, go through your closets, re-organize your basement, weed the garden, bake an apple strudel. Preoccupy your time.
4. Get off your butt and get a hobby. Do something that you love that takes time, concentration and gives you a sense of Zen or freedom. Do it every day – like writing a book for instance.
5. Say hello to the crazy cat lady! Get a pet or five. Play with them, care for them, talk to them – they are the best friends you will ever have.
6. Invite your imaginary friend's friends over.
7. Embrace the notion of alone time. Use your quiet time to restore, refuel and regenerate. Be in a solitary silence, a rest from the chaos of social mayhem.
8. Crank the K-Tel's Greatest Hits and dance in your kitchen naked. Try on your mermaid costume. Re-enact The Sound of Music with your cats. (It's best to be alone while doing these things!)
9. Connect! Go on Facebook and send one of your 346 friends a message. Go online and flirt with a potential future Mr. Lowry. Pick up the phone and call a friend. You have a great bunch of them so make it happen.
10. Reflect. Being lonely is an emotional state. You can feel lonely in a crowded room or even when you're with your best friend. It can be a feeling of not fitting in or not sharing the views of others. It can come from missing someone or feeling left out. Dig deep. Start with why you are feeling lonely.
11. Realize that you are not alone. Ever. (You know…the faeries in the chandelier…and the zombies in the basement.)

How to get over disappointment.

1. Throw a major WTF tantrum – stomp around a lot.
2. Burst into tears at the injustice of it all.
3. Curse the lives of those who you deem responsible…and those closest to them.
4. Question everything. Lose faith. Plummet downward. Crawl back up.
5. Consider that there may be a reason. Things do happen for a reason.
6. Consider the silver lining…perhaps you dodged a bullet.
7. Remember that every time a window slams down, apparently a door opens…Momism #467.
8. Get some perspective. Maybe he didn't call, maybe you didn't get the dream job, maybe you didn't get nominated for an Oscar…yet…these are first world problems.
9. Life is tough. It's the school of hard knocks…think about the lesson that's being presented.
10. Know your worth. Don't give up…give it another go!
11. You can't always get what you want…but you just might get what you need.

How to cheer yourself up.

1. Chips, wine, chocolate, Mac & cheese, pop tarts and gummy worms… in no particular order.
2. Bubble bath, lavender candle, a glass of wine, floaty music and your "rubber ducky".
3. Crank the tunes. Dance in your undies and sing at the top of your lungs! (Remember to close the curtains)
4. Sofa, blankie, popcorn, wine and movie marathon.
5. Retail therapy…from magazines to Morocco…it depends on how much cheering up you need!
6. Distract. Deny. Daydream.
7. Talk to your pet. If you don't have one, go get one. (Hamsters are low maintenance and full of fur love). Option B – watch cute animal videos.
8. Call a friend. Get out of the house. Go shopping, bowling, drinking… and other things that end in "ing."
9. Go for a walk, work out, meditate or take a nap. It's your call.
10. Find some perspective. Is it a herd of rhinos or a box of kittens?
11. Count your blessings. One bottle of wine, two bottles of wine!

Anger

How to handle anger, fury and wrath.

1. Release it. Better out than in.
2. On that note…perhaps you can write it out, walk it out, dance it out, punch the shit outta your pillow it out. Seek out a safe place to seethe.
3. Count to ten…ok one hundred. Take ten deep breaths. REPEAT this until your molecules return into your body, you stop spewing flames from your eyes and daggers from your mouth.
4. Be Buddha. Walk away. Say nothing. Be indifferent to those who seek to make you angry. Some people find malicious pleasure in trying to make you mad.
5. Think before you speak or act. Pick your battles. Choose your sword carefully. Remember that murder equals life in prison.
6. Put down the coffee pot. Step away from the potato. Scissors can't cut out pant pockets without hands in them…just saying…been there…lessons learned.
7. Don't infuse it with alcohol. Lesson learned #2.
8. Talk to someone. Just not the person who made you mad…yet…but eventually you can…once you have calmed down, rationalized your feelings and stopped wanting to cause them bodily harm.
9. Understand that life isn't fair, you can't control other people's actions, people are idiots, shit happens and sometimes they miss the bus…other times you do.
10. Defeat it with logic. Being angry, obsessing, ranting, raving and roaring isn't going to fix anything. It's only hurting you.
11. Make love, not war. Choose peace. Always remember it's your choice.

How to find patience when there isn't a drop left.

1. Clench your fists, flare your nostrils, roll your eyes back into your skull until you feel them in your throat. Bite down hard on the inside of your bottom lip until it bleeds and breathe Gawd damn it.
2. Pull out your best Oscar nominated performance and pretend that you give a shit.
3. Envision that you are part of an insane comedy show.
4. Do your best Mother Teresa impersonation and empathize with the idiot(s).
5. Accept that no one is as perfect as you and thank goodness for that because that would probably drive everyone crazy.
6. Swear prolific obscenities on the inside.
7. Take 10 deep breaths. Think 10 nice thoughts. Eat 10 pink Smarties. Are you feeling better yet? If not repeat.
8. Imagine that you will be rewarded Karmic patience points that you can turn in when you're faced with a pack of ravenous pythons, vampire vultures and a mean-spirited troll.
9. Be the Buddha. Be Gandhi. Be fucking Pollyanna.
10. Expand your capacity for tolerating stupidity, ignorance, laziness, disorganization and complete and utter disregard and disrespect for other people's time and feelings.
11. Let it be. Let it go.

Super Skills

How to process the loss of your parents.

1. Accept that it is unacceptable and know that you will never be the same. You'll go through a cesspool of emotions and you'll think it will never end or that you'll never feel alive again…but you will. You will be different – hopefully stronger and wiser – because of it.
2. You might feel frozen or paralyzed by your emotions. It will be the calm before the storm. You'll feel that nothing is real. It's an unimaginable situation and your heart and mind doesn't know any other way than to deny it. It's strange how the brain protects itself from unbearable emotional pain. Sit with it. You need time to let it settle.
3. You'll be on autopilot. You'll fake being grown up, feeling in control. You'll somehow do everything that needs to get done. Packed up, put away, buried. People may say that you're being so brave, so strong, when in fact you're feeling like a terrified abandoned lost child. Try not to pretend or rush around. The sadness won't go away any faster just by getting all the tasks done. Neither will fooling yourself that you are fine.
4. Reality will hit and you may experience, panic and regret. It comes in an OMFG moment when the armor melts away and reality sets in. They are really gone. No more hugs, chats, home cooked dinners or second chances. It's like free falling with no net. Now is a good time to reach out to friends or start grief counselling.
5. You'll be fricking mad at the whole wide frucking world. It isn't fair. Everything might make you angry and you might want to blame everyone. You may lash out, fight and question everything…it's scary but it's just the manifestation of your suffering and intensity of your love.
6. You'll be broken-hearted with a broken spirit. You may feel completely empty and void of a soul. Your emotional capacity shuts down from sheer exhaustion; you'll withdraw, close down, drift into a silent solitude to reflect, rationalize and then slowly start to rebuild.
7. Eventually you'll come to acceptance. This doesn't mean that anything is ok, but rather that you can somehow wrap your head and heart around this unthinkable truth and start to breathe again.

8. Secure your memories. Make a photo album, memory box and little shrine of your favourite keepsakes. Tuck one in your purse, keep a photo at work in your wallet, carry a card or letter, keep Dad's cufflink around or spray Mum's perfume on your pillow. Surround yourself with their presence, energy and loving memories.
9. Celebrate their life by maintaining their memory. Remember and recognize birthdays, holidays, family traditions and milestones.
10. Talk about them. Share their lives – what they taught you and what you love about them. Make them proud. Say their expressions; keep their spirits alive and celebrated.
11. Talk to them. Trust that they are never far away. Love never dies.

How to deal with family.

1. Be grateful. They brought you into this world and fed you hotdogs; they passed on genetic talents, character, freckles, curly hair, voluptuous hips and invaluable life lessons.
2. Be forgiving. After years of therapy you will realize they were only doing the best that they were capable of.
3. Appreciate them and all their quirks, idiosyncrasies, faults and failures… once they are gone, you will miss them all.
4. Learn from them. Cherish and maintain the treasures and traditions, while being mindful of the challenges, and work to adjust what might have needed a little or a lot of work.
5. Realize that The Brady Bunch, The Waltons, The Simpsons and The Cleavers are all fake families. Don't compare your family to a TV show.
6. There is no coincidence that the words dynamics and dynamite closely resemble each other.
7. Accept that family celebrations and holiday get-togethers are NEVER Hallmark moments…instead they are more like HELLMARK moments.
8. Blood is thicker than water. It's also messier.
9. There's one in every family…the black sheep, the pink sheep, the lamb and the llama.
10. Family bonds and family boundaries, you gotta love both.
11. Without them I couldn't wear the badge "Chip Off the Old Block."

How to love the meanie.

1. Find one redeemable thing to say to them – come on, just one. Umm… those are nice socks. Focus on it. See? It's not so hard.
2. Haters gonna hate. Be a lover. It takes way more energy to hold onto a negative emotion.
3. Walk in their (stinky) shoes. Just maybe they are suffering with horrible blisters.
4. Know that the drama queen is actually insanely jealously of you – so amp up your super powers and show her who's the queen bee…in the nicest of ways of course.
5. Sharpen your sarcasm sword.
6. Earn your empathy, sympathy and compassion badge for tolerating the pathetic, annoying and less socially fortunate people in the world.
7. Consider the notion of Karma. Look at it as an opportunity…a charitable gift to humankind to embrace the idiot. Share your wisdom, grasp of reality and fortitude in order to help make the world a better place.
8. OK… grow up. Ask yourself why do you even care? It seems like you do. So, why is that? Why does it feel necessary to have a hate on?
9. What would Buddha do? What would Winnie-the-Pooh do?
10. Who would you rather be? A magical loving unicorn or a fire-breathing dragon?
11. Listen to your Mother…"Kill them with kindness". You know she's right.

How to do something that you really don't want to do.

1. Ask yourself why you don't want to do it. Are you afraid? FACE YOUR FEAR! Feeling stuck? SHAKE OFF THE MUD! Bored? GET A HOBBY! Tired? GO TO BED EARLY! Addicted? GET HELP! Don't know how? LEARN! Once you figure that out – then you can take your next step.
2. Throw the infantile "I CAN'T DO THIS" hissy fit. Go on… get it out of your system. Are you done yet? Write a list of all the reasons why you can't do it. Hmm…is it a shorter list than you thought it would be? Stomp your feet, pull your hair, scream, cry, whine, complain, sulk…fine…be in denial – it's your choice.
3. Ask yourself – what do you have to lose? To gain?
4. Embrace the concept of accountability. Make a pact to follow through with a friend, mentor, the devil, Gawd or Gawddess and most importantly with yourself.
5. Take baby steps. Ok, start with crawling. Start really small and get a few "yahoo, I did its!" under your belt. You'll feel braver, stronger and more capable to tackle the big hairy monster that is next on your list.
6. Don't stop. Don't give in. You've come this far! Don't you dare quit. Commit to finishing the task like your life depends on it. Because it does. Happiness is achievable.
7. Reward yourself with gold stars.
8. Enjoy the power of showing off. Earn your "look what I did?" badge, sash and rainbow- jewelled tiara!
9. Be a domino. Create momentum. Stuff will start to happen once you get the ball rolling. Think of a happy, safe and good avalanche.
10. Give yourself a break. NOBODY is perfect. Goof-ups happen…just get back on the yellow brick road tomorrow.
11. Know that the more people you can find to help, support, encourage, inspire and be real with you, the easier your task becomes. There is power in numbers. Share the love. Return the favour. Grand slam home runs are contagious.

How to age gracefully and never grow old.

1. Never grow up.
2. Don't act your age. Age is just a number.
3. Eat healthy, exercise your body and mind, get lots of sleep and drink water and whisky.
4. Natural trumps plastic. Say no to Botox, surgery, tucks and tweaks. Real beauty is real.
5. Less is more when it comes to makeup. But more is better when it comes to micro mini-skirts.
6. Wrinkles are earned and they define a life well led. Embrace and celebrate them!
7. Attitude over longitude. You are as young as you feel. 40 is the new 30; 50 is the new 40; 60 is the new 50 and so on.
8. Keep learning and doing new things and having lots of sex!
9. Avoid fashion stereotypes, such as elastic stretchy pants, dusty rose leisure suits and orthopaedic shoes. Rock your own unique style.
10. Don't give a damn about what anyone says. You know better and you've earned it.
11. Drink from the fountain of youthful red wine.

How to be a grown-up (aka do the right thing.)

1. Practice. Practice. Practice.
2. Make mistakes. Learn from them. Make more mistakes. Learn from them again.
3. If you fall down, get up. Stand up. Show up.
4. Weigh the pros and cons of your actions. Take responsibility.
5. Think, don't just act.
6. Work on yourself. Discover yourself. Improve yourself. Polish up your shiny bits, soften the rough edges and clean out the cobwebbed corridors of your mind.
7. Recognize when you're in "child mode"; for example, when you're pulling tantrums and feeling fearful or helpless.
8. Put a little money away for a rainy day. Tsunamis do happen.
9. Say that you're sorry. Say I love you.
10. Get a job, pay your bills, learn to cook, do your own laundry. Be independent.
11. Act your age – NOT! Act like your authentic self.

Good to Know

How to get some perspective.

1. You're having a bad hair day. Well, for starters, you're lucky to have hair. If you're going bald …for the love of comb-overs just finish it off and shave it clean. If the elements play havoc with your locks or a hairdresser on crack has messed up your doo - try a ponytail, pigtails, braids, crazy gel, clips, a headband or a hat.

2. Do you hate your job? Really, who doesn't at some point? Unless you're independently wealthy or married to a sugar daddy/mama, suck it up buttercup. You have to work. What's so tragic about making money to pay for your life? How are you going to do that if you sleep in Monday to Friday? If the gig sucks so much then find a new one or find a new attitude.

3. You have a freaky family. Repeat after me: there's no such thing as a Hallmark family. From the Waltons (hello…John boy?) to the Addams Family (Cousin It)…every family has some sort of dysfunction and usually more than one curious character. Either embrace it or get therapy for it.

4. Are you feeling fat or out of shape? Stop eating chips, drinking beer and being a sloth on the sofa. Love some lettuce, grope some grapes, turn up the heat in a hot yoga class and move your sexy sloth butt…you'll feel better, your clothes will feel looser and you can hang out with real people, not only TV characters!

5. Aw, you're feeling sick. Ok it's just a cold or the flu…it's not Malaria, Leprosy or hello…Cancer. Stuff it up and cuddle up under the covers. Sip some whisky & tea, watch the soaps and drool on your pillow. I'm pretty sure that you'll live.

6. Can't scrape together any coin? Well stop spending it on stupid things. You don't need an eleventh pair of black shoes, another red lipstick or dinner out every night of the week. Start by making your lunch and dinner, shop thrift style and consider the crazy concept of saving up to pay cash for what you really want.

7. Life is messy. It's likely you'll have to deal with spills, pet barf and broken toys. Shit happens. Especially if you have pets. And what's a good party without a little spillage?! Almost everything is washable, replaceable or fixable and in the grand scheme of life it's just a thing…not a bone, a heart or a spirit.

8. Darn those bad moods. Are you feeling sad, mad and not very glad? Oh, little grasshopper…if you only lived on the ceiling, you'd never experience the grass. The beauty of feeling happy is knowing how it feels to be sad. It's gotta rain so that you can celebrate the sun.
9. Someone is late. Clocks stop, buses are delayed; give them the benefit of the doubt. Wait a little bit, daydream, window shop, grab a coffee – then split. Then agree to the 15 min rule; if they are a no show – you go. If they are perpetually late – what are you waiting for? Ditch them.
10. Someone is being a dick. Be glad that you're not them. Feel sorry for them, because they're probably miserable, hurt or they happen to be a natural born dick. Or you can simply remove yourself from their dick world or if you can't escape them (aka dick boss) then create a dick guard to protect yourself.
11. Just remember these words when you think that you're in a 911, end of the world crisis situation: "it could be worse."

How to create calm.

1. There's this thing...called breathing...I just learned how to do it right... inhale nice and slow, let the air go all the way to the bottom of your belly and then on the exhale let it blow all the magic dandelion feathers off.
2. Savour the scent of lavender. On your pillow, in your bath, on your skin, in a tea, inhale it or go for the head to toe heliotrope jumpsuit.
3. Meditate. Trust me, as someone who personifies a chipmunk on caffeine, just the notion of sitting still makes me twitch. But honestly the sedation of laying down in the dark, listening to the hypnotic drawl of a spaced-out yogi's voice is enough to put anyone's mind to sleep.
4. Medicate yourself. Whether it's Rescue Remedy, Prozac or a fine Cabernet Sauvignon...sometimes medicinal numbing is just the ticket.
5. Be in nature. Lay in the grass. Listen to the birds sing, the river babble and the wind woo. Get lost in the shape of clouds, the warmth of the sun, a cool breeze or a gin & tonic.
6. Go to your magic place. You know that place in your mind's eye where all is good and safe? The place where everything flows: the field of daisies, a Buddhist temple or your closet with a bag of chips.
7. Close your eyes. Not being able to see your boss, the person that gives you hives, the impending storm, your Visa bill, the cat barf or your flooded basement provides temporary relief.
8. Take a bubble bath with candles and wine...even more enjoyable with a "friend."
9. Tune in and tune out. From Mongolian Monks chanting and Beethoven's Moonlight Sonata to the Sex Pistol's Pretty Vacant and The Clash's Rock the Casbah...music soothes the savage soul or is it the beast?
10. Spend time with animals. Talk to squirrels. Pet random dogs on the street. Butt heads with Angus, rub Pagan's belly and let Fiend stick her tongue in your nostril.
11. Mac & Cheese, Mum's Apple Crisp, Plain Ripple chips...did someone say comfort food?

How to deal with boredom.

1. Daydream…about your dream job, dream lover, dream trip, dream purse.
2. Eat methodically. Buy a few boxes of Smarties. Line them up by colour or mix and match them in complimentary tones or create a Smartie masterpiece then devour one Smartie at a time…sucking, never crunching them of course.
3. Bored at work? Start a new hobby, like paperclip jewellery, staple art, recycled paper origami, post-it note stop animation.
4. Think up new fads…like spontaneous dance Bingo, inside out fashion, traids (3 braids).
5. Pretend that you're being interviewed by David Letterman.
6. Write the script to the movie, biography, TV show and musical of your life. Exaggerate.
7. Make up new words. Use them all day and see if people understand you. Even better, start using them. One of my faves is don't be so "banane" (benign + inane).
8. Plan your dream dinner menu.
9. Invent a new holiday, complete with traditions. For example, Dr. Seuss Day! Dress up as your fave character, eat green eggs & ham and speak in rhymes.
10. Contemplate a new look, style or hair doo. Clan of the Cave Bear meets rodeo cowgirl goes glam.
11. Get a life! There are a million fun things to do!

How to stop being a control freak.

1. Loosen the collar, belt, socks and tighty whities.
2. Stop trying to be Superman, Wonder Woman, Mother Teresa, Einstein, Jessica Rabbit and Bambi all wrapped up into one person.
3. Switch the word control with super. Then break into your best Rick James "Super Freak" impersonation.
4. Limit yourself to one anal retentive, obsessive-compulsive act a day.
5. Embrace the beauty of disorder, chaos and mayhem.
6. Step into the river and go with the flow.
7. De-alphabetize your record collection. Un-colour coordinate your closet and return your library book late. OMG!
8. Associate being hyper-organized with being hyper-annoying. Think of Elle Woods from the Legally Blonde movie.
9. Understand that the need to control is fear based. Fear of failure, anxiety, consequences, impending danger, trusting… coping. So you need to feel, deal and start to heal.
10. Repeat after me: perfection is boring.
11. World domination, becoming Queen of the Galaxy and marrying Robert Downey Jr. are unlikely…as unlikely as having control over everything in life. Make sense?

How to not cheat when dieting.

1. Get an accountability partner. Be on the hook for your actions to someone who will call you on it.
2. Get a Diet Buddy. Suffering is easier with a partner in crime and punishment.
3. Put your scale in the kitchen and weigh yourself every morning. Pay yourself $2 for every lb you lose so that you can buy yourself a new pair of jeans once you reach your goal.
4. Empty your house of all tempting treats. Don't hide them or even put them in a suitcase in the basement under lock & key…they will call to you to let them out.
5. Repeat after me…slices of cucumber are just as yummy as potato chips… they are just a lot soggier.
6. Figure out the difference between being hungry and feeling emotionally starved.
7. Hang a photo of yourself in a bikini on the fridge.
8. Eat slowly…like a hamster. Chew one pea at a time…suck on a leaf of lettuce.
9. Portion size, Barbie-sized.
10. Apparently you're most tempted to cheat late at night, when drinking alcohol and hanging out with friends…so become a boring, anti-social dweeb…NOT!
11. Screw it. Life is meant to be lived…not limited.

How to cope with a being in a drunken stupor.

1. Immediately, upon your stumble home, guzzle a gallon of water.
2. Follow this with any of the following sure-fire preventive hangover helpers: cheez-whiz hotdogs on white bread, peanut butter from the jar or a cold can of Campbell's green pea soup. It works for me.
3. Be very careful moving around – you're not stable. Perhaps take 5 on the cool linoleum floor in the kitchen…but try not to fall asleep there, it may worry your cats and they can't dial 911.
4. Crawl up the stairs. Don't look back or down, it will make you dizzy.
5. Once you make it upstairs…consider your options – bathroom or bedroom. This is a critical decision or a critical mistake.
6. If you opt for the bathroom, drink more water…or not. Assume "the position" and relinquish your sins. Experts say it's better to repent and release what evils lurk.
7. If you opt for the bedroom…try and remove your clothing and get under the covers…if that's not possible, due to tornado-style spins…grab your pillow and hit the floor.
8. Embark on an adventurous, pillow-drooling, alcohol-induced state of the sweats, spins, hallucinations, regrets and promises to never drink again sleep.
9. In the morning, drink COFFEE, BLACK. STAT.
10. If you can stomach food – Go for the Grease! Greasy eggers, greasy sausages and greasy hash browns with greasy toast.
11. Get some hair of the dog that bit ya in ya.

How to cope with a juicy cold.

1. For starters…we're not just talking about the sniffles…we're talking about the infamous tsunami cold. Every breath triggers the hairs on your body to scream in pin-needle pain, your nose is a bulbous mass of redness, you're stuffed to the gills with streaming mucous, your eyes are seeping, your ears are stinging, your throat is raw, you're dizzy and a you have a death-rattle cough that kick-starts the whole sequence of sneezing, dripping, blowing and wiping again. Yes, this is a drama worthy, 911 remedy seeking, reality.
2. Call MOM. STAT.
3. Dress for the part by wearing your dirty, sweat-soaked, germ-infested unicorn flannel pjs.
4. Consume comfort food like soft-boiled eggs, squishy white bread to wipe up the yoke and a room temperature glass of apple juice, with a side plate of ripple potato chips.
5. Ask for slow, soft head petting, reminiscent of dying infirmary patients.
6. Rub Vicks in your nose, plaster a mustard plaster on your chest and put a cool cloth on your forehead.
7. Amp up the vitamin C, D, B6, B12, Oregano Oil and Echinacea.
8. Chug Neo Citran & Gin for a deep, fever-induced comatose sleep.
9. Plan your day: sofa, blankie, box of Kleenex, chicken noodle soup with chips and all day soap operas and talk shows.
10. Take whisky for the head, sherry for the throat and snuggle Bobo Bear for the heart.
11. Indulge in lots of self-pity…because, like, seriously…you're "dying."

How to embrace exercise.

1. Try on your jeans, swimsuit or date underwear from last year.
2. Buy rainbow-sparkled, glow-in-the dark pink sneakers that match your leg warmers, headband and cape.
3. Summon your inner Richard Simons, Jane Fonda, Hercules, Zena the Warrior Princess and Bionic Woman.
4. Get creative. Try Prancercise, Dancercise or Sexercise!
5. Consider hiring a personal trainer…it works for circus animals.
6. Don't call it working out - call it making space for chips.
7. Stomp your feet in defiance, wave your arms in subordination, roll your eyes in utter revolt; it all burns calories.
8. Remind yourself how it feels when your panties creep up your bum and you had to pinch, pick, pluck and pull them back down, usually in public, in front of a gorgeous man. Trust the fact that you will never have to do that again.
9. When your perennially thin and perky Jennifer Aniston-esque trainer (who can eat anything and lose 10 lbs just by sneezing) tells you to do 10 more squats…equate sweating, pain and rigor mortis with what you'd like to do to her.
10. Imagine that you are working out in front of Robert Downey Jr.
11. Do it for the endolphins★ (endorphins, whatever).

How to save money when you are broke.

1. Take stock of the difference between need and want.
2. Use a penny (remember pennies), quarter, loonie and toonie jar. Empty your loose change into it every night.
3. Cut out the non-essentials like fashion magazines, another pair of black shoes and caviar.
4. Make a grown-up budget. Use a shoebox for rent, food, bills, household items, transportation, pets and wine.
5. Make things like lunch, dinner, clothes and gifts.
6. Recycle. Re-use. Re-build. Re-fashion. Repair. Re-gift.
7. Shop value style at Value Village, local markets and dollar stores.
8. Swap clothes, toys, books, music and skills. I'll sew you a shirt if you can cut my hair…you CAN cut hair, right?
9. Use cash. Put away the plastic.
10. Be a grown-up! Pay off your debts. Use automatic withdrawal for your bill payments. Look into RRSP's and financial investments.
11. Entertain, eat and drink at home. There is no door cover, way more grub available for less and you have choices…$15 for a glass of wine at a restaurant versus $15 to have a bottle at home. Duh.

How to rock a resumé, ace an interview and be employee of the month.

1. Stand out from the crowd. Go beyond the typical/predicable expectations. Write the movie version of your life story. Draw your designs, solve a problem, bake brownies and ice them with "Hire me".
2. Don't give up after 1 try. Bombard them with your brilliance. For instance, I sent 25 unique resume/love letters/photo scenarios (bikini snow angels)/stories/videos when I applied to work for Club Med (I got the gig btw).
3. Do your research. Know everything about the company and arrive for your interview with some new value added ideas.
4. Practice your Oscar Winning Interview performance! Write out the questions and your clever, witty and smart responses. Be ready to talk about every possible scenario.
5. Pick a great interview outfit. You might rock the fun-fur jumper but aim for the slightly more subtle look…until you are hired.
6. Brownie's Motto – Be Prepared. Bring brownies.
7. Be confident. Be you.
8. When they ask what your weakness is – answer chips. When they ask about how you work under pressure – tell them you stared down a black bear and survived two tornadoes.
9. Be versatile. Be able to wear more than one shoe, pump, flipper, snowshoe, hiking boot or racer. Make sure it's a good fit… otherwise it won't be a comfy journey in the long run.
10. Manners matter! Always send them a thank you note (Brownies don't hurt either.)
11. Once you're in – commit to permeating their space with merriment, verve and contagious inspiration…and always have a full jar of jellybeans on your desk.

How to ask your boss for a raise.

1. Anticipate, construct, prime and prepare a three week plan of attack.
2. Week 1 – Research what you're worth (a lot).
3. Week 2 – Raise the bar. (You work hard for the money – prove it).
4. Week 3 – Rehearse. (Perfect a super confident, super natural, super slam dunk spiel).
5. Write an Oscar nomination worthy, second coming of Christ, Nobel Peace Prize winning, speech that pertains to why you rock. Because you do.
6. Amp up your morning greetings. "Good morning!" "WOW, you look great." "Amazing idea!" "Damn you are smart" "Have you lost weight?" "You're the best boss ever." In other words, suck up.
7. Negotiate your raise, but have an absolutely non-negotiable range in mind. Play hardball. State your case Perry Mason style.
8. Perfect the ultimate eagle-eye, owl-ogle stare down that shows that you mean business.
9. Come back with come-back answers. Do not accept no for an answer. Smile while you shake your head in a "no response" and repeat "no" with a variety of different inflections in your voice (access your inner 2 year old…NO! NO! NO!).
10. Access your inner Samurai (keep your sword hidden). State your desired raise and shut your mouth. Be quiet. Don't say a word. Create an awkward cone of silence. Percolate positive raise vibes. Let him read your stoic gaze and fear what you are thinking, preparing. Mind warp his mind.
11. When all else fails – pull a Cuba Gooding Jr. rant: "SHOW ME THE MONEY!" Do not stop until you get what you came for.

Love

How to heal a broken heart.

1. Supply yourself with copious amounts of Kleenex, chips, chocolate, buttertarts, Mac & cheese, wine and whisky.
2. Cry, weep, sob, blubber, drip, drool, bawl, wail, yowl and howl. Because it hurts like hell.
3. Give it time. It's a loss and you have to go through it – you can't go around it. You have to feel and deal in order to heal.
4. Try not to turn your love into hate. Try to uphold your self-respect and self-esteem. Bite your tongue, delete that email and save the drama for when you are alone, with friends or your cats. Just say no to voodoo.
5. Stop stalking them. Unfriend them from Facebook. Put away the pics. Burn the t-shirt he gave you – better yet make it into the lining of your cat's litter box. Just create space. Begin to build your new life. Replace him with Robert Downey Jr. fantasies.
6. Trust that the relationship broke for a reason…and deep down you probably know why. Know there are better days and a healthier relationship ahead.
7. Wave your independence flag again. Do all the things that you love to do, but that you stopped doing "for him/her"…like watching the Bachelorette in your fun fur bunny onesie!
8. Get revenge…and I don't necessarily mean that you should cut the bottoms out of all his pants pockets…but rather by feeling complete, confident, happy and horny again.
9. Love yourself and I mean that in more ways than one.
10. Look forward to meeting the next great love of your life…because you will and you will be right back in those "date panties" again before you know it!
11. And remember that the best way to get over a man/woman is to get under another one.

How to break up with someone.

1. Whether it's a romantic relationship or a friendship have faith that ending it is what is going to serve everyone's well-being and best interests. Nothing is more disrespectful than being inauthentic and fake.
2. Choose the right time - birthdays, holidays or New Years' Eve – are not such a good idea.
3. Choose the right place - avoid public places, restaurants, streetcars and weddings.
4. Do it face-to-face never over the phone, in an email or by text message.
5. Dump with dignity and decorum. No need to go into great details about their body odor, nostril hairs or emotional impotence.
6. Get to the point. Don't dance around the deed. Don't lie. Just be straight up.
7. Be prepared for an emotional reaction – anger, shock, hysterics...or even happiness. Hold your ground; stop talking, explaining and defending your decision. Just be calm and compassionate.
8. Above all be respectful. Be honest, not hurtful.
9. Get closure. Wish them well and tell them you want them to be happy, but that you aren't the person to be able to do that.
10. Give time, time. Create some space to heal.
11. Remember that you began your relationship as friends, so aim for friendship in time.

How to survive/succeed at online dating.

1. Have zero expectations. Believe nothing that you read or see. Rule #1... online dating starts when you meet.
2. Just be aware that it's possible when he says he's 5'7", he really means that he's 5'5." Muscular build could mean jelly in the belly. Active might be that his La-Z-Boy isn't remote controlled. Re-defining his passions is code for unemployed. Not looking for anything serious...could mean that he's cheating on his wife.
3. Prepare to encounter circus freaks, midgets, chauvinists, masochists, narcissists, mamma's boys, macho men, married men, liars, drama kings, commitment phobes, drunks, parolees, psychopaths and... the needle in the haystack great guy.
4. Do not take "rejection" personally. Beauty and brains are in the eyes and minds of the beholder. You are not "invested" after "liking" someone's profile. Even if he seems perfect for you but he doesn't respond – who knows maybe he prefers big-boob, bubble-headed bimbo Barbie dolls (not that there is anything wrong with that).
5. Fortune favours the brave! Search out the boys who you fancy. Saves you from culling through 100s of emails from overweight, toothless truck drivers looking for a maid (not that there's anything wrong with that).
6. Engage in correspondence (maximum 3 emails before deciding if he is meet worthy). A – to see if he can write. B – to see if he asks you questions or only talks about himself. C – to test him with a glimpse of your true personality: I just finished making the wings for my dragonfly costume.
7. Talk on the phone before you meet. Voices say a lot – they can seduce you (Australian accent) or repulse you (Homer Simpson). It will also tell you if he can spontaneously talk and doesn't have someone else writing his emails for him.
8. Meet for coffee in a public place. Plan on 15 minutes. Trust me you will know in 5 whether it's a yay or a nay. Pre-plan a visual code (rainbow hat, daisy in the lapel, monster tee) because 10-to-1 he won't look anything like his photo and you won't be able to recognize him.

9. Buy your own coffee...even if he offers (and he better). A – because you are an independent woman and B – so he can't drug it.
10. Admit that it is awkward because it is. Signs that the date is going well: eye contact, smiles, hysterical bursts of laughter, fascinating correspondence and footsies. Signs that the date is going down the drain: his aftershave lotion is choking you, you've rolled your eyes a dozen times, the amount of Star Trek conferences he's been to doesn't impress you, he snorts out loud, burps and farts and he keeps kicking you under the table.
11. OK...it's love at first sight! You are PERFECT for each other and destined to be together forever and forever. SWOON! Really...it's lust at first sight. Go on another date just to be sure.

How to go on a date after not being on a date in ages.

1. Remember that dating is like riding a bicycle…ok maybe a unicycle.
2. Give yourself at least a day to prepare, primp, pamper, have a hair crisis, fashion crisis, a fit, change your outfit 10 times, call your friends for advice and then end up going with your first choice.
3. Date underwear 101: even if you don't plan to show off your panties… wear your Sunday best…aka *best "laid" plans*.
4. If you're nervous – take only one swig of whisky…showing up drunk, disorderly and smelling of booze may deter a second date…or not.
5. Ask questions to get them talking and find out all the deetz. Do they have a job? Where do they live? (hopefully not on their parent's couch) Are there ex-wife (s)? Where's the body buried?
6. Go easy on him. The poor guy doesn't know whether to be a knight in shining armor, a dragon slayer, the jester, king or the fool.
7. If you're doing dinner don't order spaghetti…it's way too hard to manoeuvre noodles & sauce…and bibs are so not sexy.
8. Flirt shamelessly…but be a lady.
9. Don't talk about your dream wedding.
10. Definitely kiss on the first date…this is important research.
11. Throw out the rulebook and go with your gut.

How to love yourself when you are having an "I'm fat, ugly, stupid AND a bad hair day" day.

1. Do you have hair? Consider yourself lucky. If all else fails…use barrettes, bandanas or berets…or paper bags.
2. Go for a walk with your two working legs.
3. Beautiful is as beautiful does.
4. Pull a Sally Field and realize that people really like you…regardless of your cowlick, love handles, the zit on your chin and for not knowing how to spell tchotchke (I had to look it up).
5. Hello. There are starving kids in Africa. Aids. Cancer. Flood victims. Abandoned animals. Enough said.
6. Be gentle on yourself. Realize that it's probably PMS, a full moon, post long weekend syndrome or Mercury Retrograde and that tomorrow will be a much better day.
7. Be grateful. Count your blessings. It can always be worse.
8. Think about the time that you lost your job, lost your mind, had a broken heart, broken spirit, Joe The Bunny died, or you found out Mum had a brain tumor…feeling fat all of a sudden doesn't feel so bad.
9. Spend quality time with a pet. They love to listen, they agree with everything you say, are totally empathetic, give great kisses and always give you the best advice.
10. Reach out to a friend (or ten) and return the favour on the flip side.
11. Eat KD for dinner and ripple chips for dessert, drink a bold cabernet, wear drawstring track pants and indulge in sofa surfing followed by a hot bubbly bath while listening to The Smiths.

Last but not Least

How to make Awesome Sauce.

1. Surround yourself with quirky, smart, unusual, inquisitive, bold, ballsy, open-minded, open-hearted, fun and freaky peeps.
2. Eat fear for breakfast. It's the most important meal of the day.
3. Pet, pat, hold, hug, squish, squeeze, cuddle and love any and all furry kind – especially kittens, puppies, teddy bear hamsters, bunnies, squirrels, monkeys, llamas and chipmunks.
4. Stir in some silly sauce – like wine, beer, whisky or jellybean juice!
5. Munch out on all your fave foods: cheesies, cheese & crackers, Mac & Cheese, cheese buns & cheese…get the idea?
6. Dance like no one's watching, like everyone is watching, like a fool, like a banshee. Just shake your booty, slam it, do the hop, bump & grind, do-si-do and fandango until you just can't fandango no more!
7. Dare to be different! Own your originality. Take the chance. Celebrate your YOUness.
8. WILD THING you make my heart sing! Kiss the ground, hug a tree, take a bath in a river – just for the love of G.O.D. (Great Out Doors) spend time in nature.
9. Step outside your comfort zone. Embrace something new. Wear a sparkly cape. Run, don't walk. Make a potato chip & pickle sandwich on waffles.
10. Speak your mind. Tell the truth. Always be real.
11. Celebrate, emulate, initiate and permeate ONE LOVE.

Patty-isms

Patty-isms★

Made up words and phrases with real meanings that are way more fun than the real words that inspired them.

Art of Scardiation:	The study, practice and perfection of hilarious, immature acts with the intention of scaring the bleep out of peeps.
Awesome Sauciness:	An extremely excellent attitude embodying flippy, flirty, cheeky, saucy sass.
Endolphins:	The euphoric release of happy hormones that mimic the elated joy of frolicsome dolphins.
Gawd:	The almighty, big dude/dudette, Mother earth, Greenman, supreme universal life force, idol, animal, totem, mystical, magical all powerful Oz and to infinity and beyond.
Loviation:	Infusing amplified action into the state of love creating an even bigger expression.
Lovitude:	A point of view, frame of mind, disposition and demeanour encompassing love.
Magic Moxie:	An irresistible, invincible essential super power that embodies charisma, charm, pluck, polish, pizzazz, grace, guts, vim, verve and total vixenosity★.
Mud Girl:	A depressive state of stuck in the mud, covered in heavy dirt, can't move, trapped at the bottom of a deep hole, eating worms and can't get out.

Scardiate:	The intensely hilarious, immature act of causing frightful freak-outs.
Snerney Berney:	Ecstatic, euphoric, enraptured and inspired sounds that translate into a hysterically high-pitched rhyming, nonsensical language spoken to all animals.
Spirit full:	The ethereal essence that defines your mood, morals, life force, spark and sparkle.
Wonder full:	The OMG, WOW, Holy Cow, can you believe that feeling of amazement and awe.
Vixenosity:	The coquettish realization that you're foxy.

You're a Winner!

A BONUS peek into Patty's nature and lessons learned.

1. Picture this... 7" leeches on my bum. I'm in Nepal, trekking the Annapurna Everest trail. I was on day 3 with severe dysentery that required frequent pit stops to the bush – which is where I picked up some hitchhiking leeches who were too lazy to find their own way back to the base camp. Lesson...what doesn't kill you makes you stronger.
2. There I was, taking a nap naked next to a black bear on the West Coast Trail. It was day 5, we had climbed down a rock face to wash our clothes, take a bath in the ocean, and sun-dry our skin...until Smokey the bear stumbled down the cliff, curled up beside us and fell asleep. Imagine lying perfectly still for an hour until the bear rolled over and climbed back up the rock face. Lesson...the bear didn't like our bare bottoms.
3. Just your average run-in with a herd of llamas on a very narrow path at Machu Picchu. I was dawdling behind the group on a steep incline when I heard screams up ahead – "LOOK OUT FOR THE LLAMAS!" just as I saw 7 llamas come racing down a 2-foot path. I plastered myself against the cliff only to have them stop dead in front of me. They tilted their heads and looked curiously at me and the one with the black nose licked my face. Lesson...you can fall in love anywhere.
4. I was simply spying on spiders the size of baseball mitts in Nepal. We were riding elephants in the Chitwan jungle; the guide suggests that we put on hats with heavy mesh face covers so that we can break through inch-thick webs that may disturb (anger/excite) the 12" spiders that eat birds for breakfast. Lesson...eight legs run faster than two.
5. Oh the bliss of a leisurely swim with a swarm of stinging jellyfish in Costa Rica. I was snorkelling in the most pristine, crystal clear water when all of a sudden the water felt like electrified Jello as 100s of invisible jellyfish clung to my body. Lesson...what you can't see, can hurt you.

6. Hmm…to sink or swim in the raging Big East River? Just a quick dip in an overflowing river with a friend who can't swim and forgot to put his water wings on. He was swept away…and not in a good way. He managed to hold on while I dove in, went 100 feet to the embankment, ran back to the cottage for rope, tied it to a tree and my waist, then dove back in to throw him the slack as I pulled him to safety. Lesson…life, like the river, is always half full.
7. The attack of 100 bunnies. I was at some random road stop café along the Vangroovy hwy. I pull up to refuel. The pit stop sells an enormous amount of bags of bread bits. "Why?" I ask. "Oh, to feed the rabbits, honey." I step outside, look past the parking lot to a field overrun with 1000s of rabbits. I RUN (with bags of bread in hand), lie down, and sprinkle bread all over my body as 100s of perfectly soft, nibbling wild bunnies hop, cuddle and kiss me. Lesson…heaven is real.
8. Drinking elephant poo. Elephants love playing in the water. It makes them giddy. I decide to join their bath time and was up on Jumbo's back, when he sprayed me with his trunk. He got so excited he stood on his hind legs dunking me (with my mouth open) into the filthiest poo-infested river in India. At the time it was the most fun I had ever had…2 days later the river revenge hit. Lesson…not only will an elephant never forget, neither will I.
9. Altitude sickness and midnight diarrhea at 14,000 feet. I was hiking to Machu Picchu…Dead Woman's Pass – the highest and hardest section of the trail where serious altitude dizziness and delirium kick in…especially at night in the darkest of dark as you stumble out of your tent like a sober drunk and poop your pants. Lesson…shit happens.
10. The wicked winds of the big bad Huntsville tornado. They huffed and they puffed and they blew 100s of trees down. Complete forests laid to rest. The earth turned inside out. Ancient trees snapped in two. Lesson… sometimes things have to break to be reborn.
11. Be warned about ferocious, disease-infested monkeys in Burma. I climbed 777 steps, barefoot, up to the sacred Mount Popa temple. I was told do not make eye contact, do not approach, and absolutely do not engage, touch or feed said vicious monkeys. Happily they didn't tell me not to cuddle them…as I was overtaken by adorably loveable monkeys. Lesson…Monkey see, monkey do. One love.

Made in the USA
Middletown, DE
08 June 2016